ADULT PLEASURES

DAN JACOBSON

ADULT PLEASURES
Essays on Writers and Readers

ANDRE DEUTSCH

First published 1988 by
André Deutsch Limited
105-106 Great Russell Street, London WC1B 3LJ

ISBN 0233 98204 3

Phototypeset by Falcon Graphic Art Ltd
Wallington, Surrey
Printed in Great Britain by
St Edmundsbury Press, Bury St Edmunds, Suffolk

CONTENTS

———◆———

Foreword   vii

Part One: Speculative
 1   Fantasy and Ethics   11
 2   Adult Pleasures   19
 3   A Note on 'Resistance'   26

Part Two: Byronic
 4   What's Eating Lara? (or Lord Byron's Guiltiest Secret)   31
 5   Jew d'Esprit   40
 6   Theodore Herzl   47
 7   The Brontës, Again   57

Part Three: Russian
 8   Tolstoy Young and Old   65
 9   Isaac Babel: A Jewish Cossack   71
10   Mandelstam's Widow   77
11   Sinyavsky's Art   83

Part Four: Lawrencian
12   *Women in Love* and the Death of the Will   93
13   Alpha and Omega   100
14   Up at the Ranch   107

Part Five: South African
15   Olive Schreiner   115
16   Yiddish Fiction in South Africa   129
17   The King and I   137

Acknowledgements and Bibliography   142

FOREWORD

◆

These essays have been written in two distinct phases. The first occupied a period of about fifteen years; the second, six months. During the first period I wrote in *ad hoc* fashion a large number of reviews, articles and papers for different journals and occasions. During the second, with this collection in mind, I selected certain topics on which I wanted to do more work, and which seemed to fall into recognisable groups, and did my best to see what they might make of each other and what I could make of them. The result is that something between a third and a half of this book is quite new. In a few cases the essays printed here are extended versions of what was published previously; in others, I have treated the earlier material as unceremoniously as one might treat notes or first drafts of a story. In addition, three essays have been written directly for inclusion in the collection: 'A note on "Resistance" ', 'The Brontës, Again', and (the opening paragraphs aside, which have been adapted from an earlier piece) '*Women in Love* and the Death of the Will'.

I trust the Acknowledgements and Bibliography at the back of the book, as well as references within the essays, do justice to authors whose works I have reviewed and to editors whose initial proddings and provocations were ultimately to have the effect of making a collection of this kind possible. I am also indebted to colleagues and students in the English Department, University College London, and to friends at the Australian National University, Canberra.

D.J.

PART ONE

SPECULATIVE

ONE

FANTASY AND ETHICS

———◆———

If, as we are usually asked to believe, great literature has a morally improving effect on us, why is it so preoccupied with presenting to us behaviour of a morally deplorable kind?

This question takes us back, in effect, to *The Republic*. Two of the reasons Plato advances for objecting to having poets and poetry in his ideal polity are relevant here. The first is that poets are liars: they tell stories which they know to be untrue, and they make claims to expert or professional knowledge which they do not have. The second is that poets present to their readers bad models of behaviour; models from which it is possible to learn only wrongdoing. For example, Plato says, they show the gods behaving viciously and irresponsibly; they describe the deeds of bad fathers and bad governors instead of good ones.

They are still at it, as we all know. It is universally admitted (outside the Peoples' Republics, at any rate) that novelists, poets, and playwrights are on the whole much more successful at writing about the misguided, the wicked, and the unhappy than they are at writing about the virtuous and the happy. Even the virtuous and unhappy usually seem to defeat them. Yet relatively few of the moral zealots of criticism appear to see these facts as a direct challenge to the convictions they hold about the likely effects of good literature on those who are exposed to it.

Plato's objections to poetry have of course evoked answers of various kinds down the years. One counter-argument which has been put with a greater or lesser degree of subtlety by different writers is to say that while poets do present us with many vivid illustrations of bad behaviour, they also show us that behaviour getting its just desserts. The bad men in literature, unlike all too many bad men in life, are comprehensively punished for their evil-doing. Indeed, in literature one finds many examples of men who are not *really* bad being punished for committing bad actions inadvertently (Oedipus), or for allowing all their actions to be determined by a single moral failing (Macbeth, Hamlet). Watching this process, watching men who are so much like ourselves suffer so greatly for

11

their faults – says Aristotle – we feel pity and terror; and it is in or through the purging of these emotions that tragedy works beneficially on us.

The arguments which have been roughly compressed into one another in the previous paragraph actually address themselves to two related but separate issues or parts of ourselves. The one sees the moral effect of literature in terms of the warnings it proclaims and the lessons it carries. Crime, it shows us, does not pay; virtue is rewarded – at least by the admiration of the poet, if not in any more tangible fashion. Aristotle on the other hand speaks of the state of mind or psychological condition induced in us by watching tragedy; and it is that which he commends to us.

*

Leaving these remarks hanging in the air for the time being, I would like to go on to make some others of an even more general kind about the nature of fantasy. What I have in mind here are not the highly elaborated fantasies of literature, but the commonplace, humble fantasies about ourselves and others in which we all indulge, willy-nilly, in the course of everyday life.

Ordinarily we think of our fantasies or day-dreams as a means through which we take brief, interior holidays from the compulsions and frustrations which inevitably make up much of our experience. Confronted with all the unwelcome exigencies of life – losses, failures, insufficiencies, deprivations, conflicts between irreconcilable desires – we have recourse to a silent, instantly available source of imaginary gratification. However fleetingly, and in however fragmentary a fashion, we create through our fantasies a world in which things, people, and we ourselves either are as we wish them to be, or can readily be made to become so. Everyone inside his own head occasionally plays at being Superman; and he feels the need to do so precisely because he is not Superman. To put the point in another way: if it is difficult to conceive of an immortal, omniscient, and omnipotent being who has a fantasy life (what need would he have for it? what would he do with it?), it is impossible to imagine how creatures like ourselves, who are endowed with consciousness, and hence with a consciousness of our limitations, could survive without one.

Escape, then, from the innumerable internal and external constraints which bind us is certainly one of the prime functions of fantasy. Looked at from another point of view, however, fantasy can be thought of as the *creator* of some of the constraints – some of the moral constraints, at least – from which it seems to offer us a temporary release.

How can this be? How can the one activity be said to have such contradictory effects or consequences? Well, at the very heart of the moral life, of all ethical judgements, of our notions of right or wrong action and feeling, and, beneath or beyond these, of our sense not merely of what is permissible but of what is possible for ourselves and others, there lies an awareness of the reality of other people's lives to *them*: the incredible yet ineluctable fact that they are as much 'centres of self' (to use George Eliot's phrase) to themselves as I am to myself. The power which enables us to apprehend others in this way is that of the imagination: we can arrive at such an apprehension of them only by 'putting ourselves in their place', as we say, or by 'putting them in our place'. Indeed, so interdependent are we, as social animals, that this exercise of the imaginative powers is actually the foundation of our own sense of ourselves: of who or what we are, and of what we hope or fear we may become.

The entire activity, in other words, is native to the mind and is largely involuntary in its functioning. The fact that some people appear to be 'better' at it than others does not really affect the issue. Only in certain psychopathic or autistic states – states which are considered to be psychopathic or autistic for that very reason – does it appear to be completely dormant. From infancy onwards we are engaged in a constant movement out of our own minds, or what we believe to be our own minds, into a swift, tentative, rapidly relinquished possession of the minds of others, or what we believe to be their minds, and then back into ourselves. We do it all the time; we do it even when we do not know that we are doing it; every act of speculation about the motives and actions of the people around us, and about their responses to ours, is just another form of it. Indeed, every time we manage to get ourselves across a street crowded with traffic and pedestrians we have made literally innumerable and immeasureable (in terms of duration) forays in and out of our consciousness and the consciousness of others. So humble and continuous, ultimately, is the activity I am speaking of; and so vital to our survival.

Yet all this, to which I initially gave the elevated title of 'the exercise of our imaginative powers', is not only close to that other private, consolatory, and apparently self-centred mode of fantasy described earlier, but in many respects is virtually indistinguishable from it. So far from the 'self-centred' fantasies being diametrically opposed in their origins and effects to the 'other-centred' fantasies, so far from each kind inhabiting and animating a different area or level of the self, the fact is that they are continuous with one another; neither kind is conceivable without the other. We can only put ourselves in somebody else's place because of a need or desire (a need which is a desire) to imagine or to pretend that we are that person, and hence that we are no longer ourselves; we can only put somebody else in our place because we need or desire to imagine him there. At what point in this process, exactly, does 'escape' turn into 'constraint', and vice-versa?

To ask the question is to answer it; or rather, to realise that it is one which cannot be answered. The mental and emotional activities I have tried to describe not only enable us to cross the street safely, or to learn from others how to do it; it is in them, and through them, and because of them that we are able to feel compassion for one another; our capacity for sexual arousal depends heavily on them; because of them we have an instinct or hunger, which is almost as deep as any within us, for justice and fair-dealing; because of them we are capable of being moved to admiration or wonder at the achievements of others. However, we must not suppose that it is possible for our fantasies, in all their complexity and urgency, to humanise and moralise us in one direction only, so to speak. The more vividly we see others *as* other, responsive primarily to their own needs and answerable to themselves, the greater the threat to us, or at least the pressure on us, which we may feel to be emanating from them. (And the more persistently we may therefore be driven back into fantasies of exercising power over them, doing away with them, or simply doing without them.) It is because we are compelled in fantasy to inhabit the minds and nervous systems of others, and have them inhabit ours, that we are capable of taking pleasure in the pains they suffer, or in the humiliations they endure, or indeed in the humiliations we inflict on them. Sadism is as 'imaginative' in this sense as compassion; envy as imaginative as admiration. In this respect the capacity for sympathy is rather like the gift of speech itself: once we are endowed with it, it is always open to us to use it for the telling of lies as well as for the telling of truth. Our ability to feel simultaneously many contradictory, complicated emotions is in large part both the result of our fantasy-life, and the reason why we have so urgent a need to try to imagine ourselves simpler and more straightforward than we are.

The borderline between fantasy and the moral consciousness is, therefore, everywhere and nowhere. Neither could exist without the other. Notwithstanding the fact that they are usually spoken about in such different terms (the moral consciousness being adult, subject to the will, etc.; fantasy being childish, weak, self-destructive), nothing could be more mistaken than to regard them as belonging to domains which are only loosely or adventitiously connected. The relations between them are never fixed into a simple pattern of impulse (fantasy) and rebuke (moral consciousness), or escape (fantasy) and constraint (moral consciousness). The mutal exchanges, impersonations, and interpenetrations in which they are engaged are never-ending. (Hence, among much else, the anxieties of our fantasy-life; not to speak of the pleasures of moral passion.) It could not be otherwise, given the paradoxical, 'reality-creating' function which, *malgré eux* and *malgré nous* in many cases, our fantasies perform. The more complicated they become, the greater is the degree of anxiety they are likely to arouse; eventually we may arrive at a point at which they themselves become that from which we feel the need to escape as best we can. Neurotic, self-hurtful fantasies are clearly a case in point; so are the compulsive states of reverie and the irreversible chains of thought in which some people periodically find themselves locked; so perhaps are nightmares.

*

An obvious and overwhelming difference between works of literature and the random, truncated, and indispensable fantasies of day-to-day (and night-to-night) existence is the degree of organisation which marks the former. These have a beginning and end; their form and their content stand in a reciprocal, mutually explanatory relationship to one another; the tensions which produced them, and which they produce, are, ideally speaking, the tensions which they themselves express and resolve. Yet it is possible to see this overall coherence of the literary work as a function of yet another crucial and even more deep-lying difference between the fantasies of literature and those of our private lives. Unlike our ordinary fantasies, the literary work is an enterprise which is *voluntarily* embarked on and carried through both by its creator and its reader or spectator. It seems to me not just reasonable but necessary to assume that the work is capable of development and elaboration, and of being carried through to a conclusion, and hence of being made accessible to others, precisely because it arises as a result of an act of choice on the part of the writer. Then the reader or spectator makes a parallel act of choice on his side.

True, the writer may feel that he has no alternative but to devote himself to the story or poem pressing on his consciousness; the reader may be so gripped by the work that he 'can't put it down', to use the common, revealing phrase. Nevertheless, I am convinced that one of the greatest of the many services which imaginative writing of all kinds performs for us is simply to give us the power to choose whether or not to be involved in the fantasy-worlds which it creates. We do not really have such a choice with our quotidian fantasies; even the most indulgent and wishful of them (or perhaps those especially) surface without our volition; the others come and go so rapidly and constantly we can hardly be conscious of them as imaginative acts on which our lives depend. By contrast, the consciousness of our power to choose is continuous throughout our exposure to any poem or story we read, or any play we attend, and is an important element of our response to it. In rather the same terms, something of the same sort can be said of the writer's involvement with a work which he himself is creating. One might say of him that he has transformed a compulsion into a choice. The sense of 'escape' which literature offers us begins to operate, therefore, far earlier and at a more primitive level than is commonly supposed. To have a choice as to whether or not we shall enter into this or that fantasy is *itself* an escape from the conditions which ordinarily govern our lives.

Like any other fantasy, the literary work speaks to us as best it can of the undischarged and ultimately undischargeable desires which have brought it into existence. That is the secret of its power, and (as it were) the secret of its sorrow as well. Like any other fantasy it not only 'shifts' anxiety, but rouses it as well.*
Unlike any other fantasy, however, the literary work does not permit these latter or reflexive anxieties to disrupt it, or to abbreviate it, or to turn it in some wholly new direction, or to fix it in a helpless, repetitive to-and-fro movement of mind and emotion. On the contrary: the development and elaboration of the fantasy

---

* Perhaps the simplest expression of this kind of aroused or secondary anxiety, as we ordinarily experience it, is the asking of ourselves such questions as: 'What's the matter with me? Why don't I get on with my life, instead of day-dreaming it away . . .?'

which I referred to earlier is achieved precisely *by its incorporating as many of such self-generated anxieties as it can.* That is how it achieves a wholeness or autonomy unattainable by any other means. That is why it returns us to the unconscious or half-conscious states in which our moral sense is constantly coming to birth. In choosing to enter this process, whether as writers or readers, we are taken not beyond good and evil, as Nietzsche's aesthetic would have it, but to the sources of both.

We do not return to them as we ordinarily do: under compulsion, driven as much by habit and prepossession and a determination to remain what we already believe ourselves to be as by the need to imagine ourselves and our neighbours anew. We go there freely and with our eyes open; we go there unalarmed, because we know that the trials of the experience will be resolved to our satisfaction. And if they are not, we can always close the book or walk out of the theatre and forget about them. Which is more than we can do with all the other barely formed, barely known imaginings within us. We have no choice but to keep them going because they, in the end, are what keep us going.

*

And ethics? And instruction? And models of behaviour? Well, implicit in what I have said is the belief that the internal action or plot of the story or poem, in all its manifestations, contains, reveals, and indeed in large part *is* the drama of the writer's relationship to his unfolding conception. Implicit in it, too, is the belief that one of the things we do when we read the work is to enact on our side an analogous drama: the drama of our relationship to what has been unfolded. That sounds complicated, and it is complicated; but we do it readily enough; and if we ever learn anything from the work it is primarily because it enables us to go from beginning to end through such a series of experiences and enactments. *They* are its essential 'meaning': not anything extractable from it *post hoc*, in the form of ethical instruction, sociological insight, witting or unwitting ideological self-definition, or, for that matter, philosophic truth.

The fact that Macbeth and Othello come in their different ways to a sticky end is clearly important to the overall effect of *Macbeth* and *Othello*. But if, in our search for ethical instruction, we choose to look on the punishment finally meted out to them as the revelation of the essential moral burden of the plays, it seems to me we have gone a long way down the road to agreeing with the celebrated conclusions of Thomas Rymer, the eighteenth-century critic, who discovered the moral of *Othello* to be (a) that you should never allow your daughter to marry a blackamoor, and (b) that if, despite your efforts, she does contract such a marriage, then let her be careful about counting her linen. If we are trying to account in broad terms for the effects which the conclusion of the play has on us, we must recognise that almost as important to it as Othello's guilt and remorse is Iago's guilt and lack of remorse, and quite as important as the guilt of them both is ours. By this I do not mean only the misgivings we may have brought to the

16

theatre about our own jealousies, say, or about our ambitions to manipulate others; but also the pleasurable or 'artful' guilt we have acquired by choosing to watch, for our amusement, these creatures of fantasy go through the torments of the particular passions which agitate them. And what applies to us has already applied, in different but comparable measure, to the author. Of the pressures and ambivalences of all kinds which he felt – those he brought to the project and those which its execution roused in him – the play itself is the record.

But let me try to illustrate the processes I have described not by invoking the action of a tragedy on that scale, but by means of a single, comic, incident in one of the novels of Jane Austen. It will serve the purpose just as well – and that in itself is a critical point worth making. There is a famous scene in *Emma*, in which the heroine makes ill-natured fun of a foolish, babbling, impoverished spinster, Miss Bates. She and Emma, together with various others, have been on a picnic which has not gone off quite as Emma would have wished it to do. Now there is a pause in the proceedings. To fill it in someone makes the suggestion that they should play a game: everybody should say one thing very clever, or two things moderately clever, or three things very dull. Miss Bates exclaims that the last option will suit her well enough; she does it every time she opens her mouth. Whereupon Emma jumps in: 'Ah! Ma'am, but there may be a difficulty. Pardon me, but you will be limited as to number – only three at once.' It takes Miss Bates a little time to understand the insult: 'but when it burst on her, it could not anger, though a slight blush showed that it could pain her.' Later, as the picnic breaks up, Emma is severely rebuked for her unkindness by Mr Knightley, the man who loves her.

The entire scene is often alluded to, quite understandably, as an example of the scrupulosity of conscience which accompanies and deepens Jane Austen's sense of comedy. Yet even as we acknowledge the justice of Mr Knightley's rebuke of Emma we are entitled to ask (though I have never actually seen it done): but who has been making mock of poor Miss Bates over some three hundred pages if not the novelist herself? Only now, in order to discomfit Emma, she sharply reminds her that Miss Bates has a 'centre of self' which is capable of being wounded, and that out of sheer wantonness she has succeeded in wounding it. In other words, the aggression and impatience which have contributed to the comic portrait of Miss Bates – and which Jane Austen has vented behind Miss Bates's back, as it were, for Miss Bates does not know that she is a character in a novel, and that Jane Austen has put in her mouth every imbecilic thing she says – Emma is compelled by her creator to express in directly wounding fashion, face to face; then she is promptly chastised for doing it. Moreover, we cannot become aware of Emma's discomfiture without realising that she is not the only target in the author's sights. The sense of amused superiority to Miss Bates, and the sympathy with Emma's wit and high spirits which Jane Austen has fostered in us, are suddenly shown up as a form of callousness. Our complacency is transformed into compunction; while the author's compunction about her character licenses her, in effect, to make this sally against us. 'It was badly done, indeed!' cries Mr Knightley to Emma. What should we cry to the novelist?

We have no choice: we can only cry that it has been well done, indeed. It is out of such instantaneous but decisive contractions and compactions of feeling taking place within the author, and therefore within her work, such reversals and diversions of sympathy and hostility, that novels are written.

It is also for the sake of them that they are read. In this particular instance it is much to the point that Emma should initially try to turn Mr Knightley aside by saying that Miss Bates was too stupid to understand what had been said against her: she is still trying to deny the unwelcome relevation which has just been made to her of Miss Bates's 'centre of self'. It is also to the point that in the course of his rebuke Mr Knightley should remind Emma of what Miss Bates had been to her during her childhood: that is, during the period when the dividing line between fantasy and reality is hardest to discern, and when the most significant and longest-lasting features of our moral consciousness are determined.

One can take the case of *Emma* a stage further by pointing out that the action of the novel consists essentially of the heroine learning painfully that her plans to determine the destinies of the people around her, by successively matching them to the men and women she chooses on their behalf, are misguided and self-defeating. No one, she discovers, after a thoroughgoing chastisement at the hands of her creator, has the wisdom to make such plans for others.

No one, that is, except the novelist herself. In the course of the book Jane Austen naturally manages to marry off everyone in it, Emma included, to the most appropriate person. And in what terms does she speak of Emma's amateur essays in the craft? 'The *insufferable vanity* of believing herself in the secret of everybody's feelings, the *unpardonable arrogance* of proposing to arrange everyone's destiny.' (My italics.)

It is a wonderfully bold, reflexive remark. In her portrait of bossy, fantasising Emma is Jane Austen punishing or rewarding herself for being a novelist? (She is certainly laughing at herself, I think, though not without a certain degree of bitterness.) Are words like 'reward' and 'punish' adequate to the complexity and intensity of the psychic processes involved? Have I succeeded in making clearer how swiftly and in what unexpected ways our fantasies must breed upon themselves if they are ever to become adequate to all the selves which each of us is?

TWO

ADULT PLEASURES

———◆———

Poets, Shelley wrote, are the unacknowledged legislators of the world. The quotation is embarrassingly well known. Few of those who invoke it, however, seem much embarrassed by the fact that Shelley's proclamation was made just at the time when an unprecedented gap was beginning to open up between poets and other imaginative writers, as a class, and the rulers of the society they lived in. Milton, Marvell, Dryden, Chaucer, even Shakespeare (to confine oneself to some obvious instances among Shelley's predecessors in England) had intimate connections with one or another circle in the court or parliament of their time, and in different ways identified themselves profoundly with the personal and political aspirations of the leaders of those circles. By Shelley's day, as a result of social transformations of which he was acutely aware, all that was gone. Indeed, the claim he makes on behalf of himself and his fellows clearly suggests as much. Poets are the *unacknowledged* legislators of the world: which is to say that their work as legislators is done in secret; it is done in opposition; it is done in a mode which is beyond the comprehension, let alone the sympathy, of the public or authorised legislators. The 'mechanists and reasoners', as he calls the rulers of his era, had shown themselves to be incapable of instructing mankind in its feelings, of developing its sensibilities, of creating a world which is spiritually inhabitable. So it was up to someone else to take up the task.

And now? The more any professional or intellectual group feels itself threatened, the more extravagant become the claims it is likely to make about its importance in the general scheme of things. Poets, dramatists, and novelists are not immune from this tendency; nor are critics; nor are professors of literature in the universities. For many years now members of these connected and sometimes overlapping groups have been telling us, in quasi-Shelleyan terms, that their activity is chiefly to be valued as a kind of diagnostic or seismographic record of movements within entire cultures or phases of civilisation. ('Poets', Shelley wrote, again in his 'Defence of Poetry', 'are the mirrors of the gigantic shadows which futurity casts upon the present.') The imaginative writer has the power to

19

apprehend directly the inner dynamics of his society and to reveal to us, sometimes knowingly, sometimes unconsciously, the true nature of the moral, psychological, and political processes which sustain it. It follows that he also has at his disposal – or perhaps they have him at their disposal – prophetic insights about the direction in which we are being driven by those processes.

Many assumptions are buried within these claims; two in particular are worth looking at immediately. The first is that society at large, or even an entire civilisation, should ultimately be understood as a unity or totality. Its institutions and actions, its art and politics, are revelatory not just of themselves, or even of each other, but of the whole to which they belong. (Just as the deeds, habits, and speech-patterns of a person may all be seen as manifestations of his underlying 'character'.) This appears to be indispensable to the sociological or anthropological way of looking at society, and we should not be surprised to find it so unquestionably in the ascendant among literary people. The second assumption is a historicist or deterministic one. If the writer has the power to tell us in which direction we are being driven, then the future which he discerns must already somehow be in existence; it has to be there, waiting for us, or he could not sense it.

A half-acknowledged determinism of the same kind appears perhaps even more strongly in the familiar image of the writer as 'the antennae of the race': a figure which one comes across frequently in editorials on the importance of literature in contemporary life, or in statements issued by arts councils to accompany their benefactions. Here the writer does not merely 'mirror' the future, as in Shelley's phrase, but actually feels his way into it, or over it, and warns the rest of us (who presumably make up the body of the beetle, dragging on behind) what lies ahead. Or perhaps, since the word 'antennae' has acquired such a strong, additional meaning over the last few decades, the artist is conceived by some of those who use the phrase as a kind of highly specialised tracking station, forever scanning deep space for the missiles which at this very moment are hurtling directly towards us.

Important tasks, these are; no question about it. It is not surprising that (since the Romantic revolution, at least) writers have generally managed to overcome their natural modesty and have brought themselves to agree that yes, they do seem to be peculiarly well fitted to serve as the true heirs of the prophets, as the diviners of the spirit of the age, as the begetters of the feelings which will carry us through our present spiritual crises, as the diagnosticians of the deep ailments of our psyches. 'The priest departs, the divine literatus comes!' exulted Walt Whitman in *Democratic Vistas*, managing in his usual fashion to provoke a maximum degree of embarrassment with the smallest number of words. He was actually somewhat premature in making this claim: the priests have by no means obligingly vacated the scene, and as a dispenser of prophetic wisdom the writer has to compete also with ever-growing numbers of historians, philosophers, and television personalities. Not to mention some divine social scientists. Nevertheless, what we are asked to believe, when such claims are made, is that the *kind* of truth we can deduce from the writer's work, if we respond to it with the seriousness it deserves, ultimately resembles that to be found in the utterances of those, like priests, social scientists and philosophers, whose enquiries into human affairs are conducted in a very different spirit from his own.

The writer, it is suggested, is able to provide us with some of the truths he has to offer because of his direct poetic or novelistic or dramatic engagement with the major 'issues' of the day: the position of women in modern society, say, or the decline of religious faith, or the fact that for the first time in history mankind now has the power to put an end to itself. Alternatively, he can deliver his truth indirectly, without knowing that he is doing so, or even in contradiction to his own understanding of what he is about and his audience's perception of what they are responding to. (Then it is up to the critic to show how crucial an element in the transmission of the truth is the writer's failure to comprehend fully just what he was doing.) Either way, what will be shown to matter most in the work is precisely that which can be extracted from it in the form of 'usable' insight into the society's conscious or unconscious preoccupations: ideological or philosophical or moral or historical, as the case may be. It is these insights which determine the intellectual worth of the work; they are the lumps of valuable ore which remain in the pan when everything else, the dross of the adventitious and arbitrary, has been washed away.

*

Every age has its own particular forms of philistinism, which it finds almost impossible to recognise as such. How difficult it is in our own case to believe that a critical approach which apparently does literature so much honour, which treats literary works as the nearest thing we have to scriptures and oracles, can itself be philistine; indifferent to art, even hostile to it. It is especially difficult for writers to accept that this may be so when they are the beneficiaries, materially and psychically, of that impulse.

But whether they are the beneficiaries artistically is another matter. Some of my scepticism on this score springs, I must admit, from a recollection of my too-ready acceptance, years ago, of certain notions to be found in modernist literature which I was invited to think of as genuine modes of historical analysis or explanation: genuine diagnoses, in fact. I am thinking here, for instance, of T.S. Eliot's running together of sexual sterility and a decline in religious faith, in *The Waste Land*, as if the one were bound to lead to the other, or at least could be recognised as a symptom of the other. (And Eliot's backing away from what he had done, his talk of *The Waste Land* as a 'personal grouse' could hardly controvert the evidence of the poem itself.) Another instance would be Lawrence's assertions (in *Women in Love* and elsewhere) that a hypertrophied 'will' was at the root of some of the most catastrophic developments of the century.* However, I should add that still more of my scepticism springs from the fact that I now value *The Waste Land* and *Women in Love* almost as much as I did in the past, when teachers, critics, and (not least) the writers themselves seemed to demand from me some kind of literal assent to the 'doctrine' these works presented.

If that is gone, what has replaced it? I shall try to answer that question, in a general way, shortly. Before doing so, however, I have to make a number of far-reaching concessions in favour of the assumptions and expectations I claim to be so dubious about. First of all, as parts of our mental equipment they are to all intents and purposes ineradicable; they cannot be expelled by an effort of will. Once they are held by both writers and readers, they are bound to determine how books are written and how they are read, and no regrets or chidings will alter this state of affairs.

Secondly (and this is not quite the same point as the one made just above), all our communications with one another are reflexive: by which I mean that right or wrong, true or false, they will have consequences both on those who initiate them and on those who attend to them. Witness the case of Byron, which is discussed in an essay below, and his effect on his contemporaries and successors. Or, to take a far more spectacular instance, witness the biblical prophets, who are so often approvingly cited as forerunners of and exemplars to our own writers of fiction and verse. (Though fiction was the one thing the prophets did *not* believe they were writing.) If the prophets were 'wrong', as I believe them to have been, in their understanding of what led to the defeat of the ancient states of Israel and Judah by the forces of the Assyrians and Babylonians; if that defeat had nothing to do with the wrath of Jehovah and the sins of the people of Israel, and everything to do with the military power of great riverine states – so what? The *effect* that the prophets' diagnostic 'error' was ultimately to have on the course of world history remains of incomparably greater importance than anything the Assyrians and Babylonians themselves managed to produce. In other words, by securing our assent to their descriptions of what is happening to us, our writers do crucially help to shape both our past and future.

Thirdly, of course any writer – biblical, ancient, and modern – speaks through and within the constraints imposed on him by the language he uses and the traditions he has inherited. His work is engendered by such constraints and limited by them; it questions them and embodies them. Inevitably, his successors will be able to perceive the lineaments and articulate the modes of operation of some of these more easily than he himself ever could; and the same in turn will apply to the successors, and to those who succeed them . . . and so on and on. Thus 'expression' must alter with 'sensibility', to quote Eliot's cautious formulation, and 'sensibility alters from generation to generation, whether we will or no'. In examining and trying to classify such alterations – and where will they be

* See '*Women in Love* and the Death of the Will' below.

revealed more clearly than in literature? – we can hope to come to a better understanding of ourselves and of the past: hardly a disreputable objective for us to set ourselves.

Finally, it must be said that there are many societies, even nations, which would barely have come into existence, or which would have had no moral and political life worth contemplating, if it had not been for their writers. To illustrate what I mean here I do not need to point towards Central and Eastern Europe, and the 'alternative governments' which writers there have constituted for so long: the Afrikaner nationalist movement in my native South Africa would have been unimaginable without the claims made for both the people and the language by the earliest writers in Afrikaans, and the poems and essays they produced to substantiate those claims.

*

After all of which – what remains of my scepticism about the idea of the writer as prophet and unacknowledged legislator of mankind? The only answer I can give to this question is: a belief that the real teaching which an imaginative work offers us, the very source of whatever truth it contains, is the pleasure we get out of it. It is *there*, in that experience, one which cannot be transposed into or mistaken for any other, that the moral and intellectual value of the work is to be found; and if it is not there, it is nowhere.

True, the teaching (diagnosing, legislating, elevating) function of literature has always been thought to run inextricably together with that of giving pleasure. But that does not meet the point I am making here. Nor am I interested in arguing that the pleasure given by the work is 'more important' than the instruction it offers, or comes first in our response to it (however painful may be the material it deals with). Even to say that there is nothing instrumental about that pleasure, and that it is not subordinate to any other end, does not seem to me to go far enough. The trouble with all such formulations is that they express and perpetuate the very bifurcation between teaching and pleasure I am objecting to, and all that follows from it, and they thus falsify the central issue or at least make it harder to see. Rather than follow up such dead trails, I would suggest that we badly need to expand our vocabulary when it comes to describing our intellectual pleasures. For they, it turns out, can be more urgent and adult than most of the beliefs and attitudes by which we ordinarily identify ourselves; not to speak of the transferable and generalisable lessons we are so eager to derive from the work of others.

Let me put the argument in quite different terms. It is not and never can be the ebb and flow of events outside a novel or poem (great historical events, little biographical events, 'movements', issues, trends, changes in sensibility, and all the rest) which most searchingly examine the assertions and implications of any kind which it contains. All these matter less to it than the ebb and flow of the events in the story or poem itself. Its power lies in the fact that every element of which it is constituted, from the largest development of its plot or story to the tiniest inflection of its rhythm, is itself an 'event', which comments on every other and is in turn commented on by every other. Each draws something from, and expresses something of, all the warring ideas and ambitions of the writer: many of which he can acknowledge and repudiate in no form other than that given to him by his art. Ideally speaking, in a work of literature there are no privileged areas – even if the author himself tries to set them up – which are protected from the reciprocal or fluctuating processes just described, or which are entitled to special consideration by virtue of the topics they comprehend or the assertions they contain. Indeed, the greater the work, the less it will permit the assertions made within it, in any form, to stand free from itself; the more it will resist declarations of independence by any of its parts. What is more it will never resist them so fiercely as when the writer himself would rather it did not. And that resistance is itself another source of the pleasure it gives to him and to us.

Paradoxically, the inflated romantic and post-romantic expectations of the writer spoken of earlier are merely an inversion of certain older and perhaps less flattering expectations that he will get on with the job of celebrating the emergence of a particular social and political order, and will conscientiously 'prophesy' its continuance into the indefinite future. (As Virgil did with the birth of empire, say, or Shakespeare did with the birth of Elizabeth in *Henry VIII*.) The resemblance between these two sets of expectations – the moderns taking it for granted that the activity of the writer will on the whole be subversive of the existing order, the ancients more or less assuming that he will support it – should not really come as a surprise. Both look to literature to provide truths which will somehow 'stand free' of the work in which they appear; both wish to diminish the possibility of its containing other kinds of truth or illustrating other modes of truth-telling.

How are these to be identified with the pleasure the work gives? In this way, I believe. In life, most of the conflicts we go through are forced upon us, or appear to have been forced upon us; we would prefer to have things go all our own way, if only we could so arrange them, and if only we could discover what we really wish 'our way' to be; we suffer every time we are worsted, and perhaps we never suffer more than when we suspect that it is we ourselves who have done the worsting. In art of any consequence a strange reversal takes place. There the conflict is willingly embraced: the artist chooses freely to pit against each other his longings for himself and what he knows of the longings of others; and against them in turn he pits whatever he has felt of the weight and momentum of the world, its obduracy and its indifference to him. For fun! For the pleasure of it! What he comes to realise then (and his readers with him) is that among the deepest of our desires is to feel the weight and obduracy of the world as if they were all our own, and all we have.

Of course most writers hold passionate convictions on all sorts of subjects. Of course they are driven by motives of which they may know little, consciously, and by historical and intellectual forces which are ultimately beyond their comprehension. What makes the work matter – which is to say, what makes it enjoyable – is the resistance it puts up to them.

THREE

A NOTE ON 'RESISTANCE'

In the last essay the word 'resistance' was used to refer both to the internal connections between the parts of a poem or story, and to the relation which the author has with the work as a whole. The distinction between these uses is in fact more apparent than real. Both refer to the antagonistic yet secretly complicit energies which are released in the work, and whose dramatic interactions make up its form and give it its substance.

What I want to do here is to extend the scope of the term by applying it too to the reader's experience. In the two previous essays I argued that his response to the work takes the form, effectively, of a 'miming' of the processes the writer went through in producing it. Like the writer's, his sympathies have to be torn in order to be re-united; his needs roused so that their contradictions might be at once made apparent and (provisionally) resolved. Only in the arena provided by the imaginative work, and only to the extent to which he participates in its interactions, can this be done.

But if we were to shift this response a stage back, or a stage deeper, what then? On the one hand, the reader has chosen to take possession of the story or poem; on the other hand, it wants to take possession of him. Certainly he is agreeable, even eager, for it to do so; but he is incapable of leaving behind him all his habits of mind and sensibility, and it would say precious little to him if he did. Rather as the writer discovers that the work never 'comes out' quite as he imagined it might; that what it wants to say is not necessarily what he wanted to say (or thought he wanted to say); and that the formal demands it makes of him, and the questions about himself which it raises, are not those he anticipated – so, in comparable fashion, the reader discovers that, irrespective of his needs, the work demands of him that he read it on *its* terms, in the context of *its* prepossessions. And just as there is nothing in the act of writing quite so thrilling and exasperating for the writer as discovering how recalcitrant to his own prior suppositions a work can be, so a reader may come to value it most for its differentness from anything he himself is or believes he wants to be.

26

Even among our pleasures or relaxations, in other words, there is no pleasure as keen as that of seeking resistance in order to overcome it, or of creating tension in order to discharge it. Hence the appeal of art, of games, and of sexual activity; not to speak of those strange areas in which all three seem to meet and merge. Witness the following description of young Hanno's piano-playing in Thomas Mann's *Buddenbrooks*, to which these remarks owe more than I can easily say:

> He denied himself and his audience the resolution; he kept it back. What would it be, this resolution, this enchanting, satisfying absorption into the B major chord? A joy beyond compare, a gratification of overpowering sweetness. Peace! Bliss! The kingdom of heaven; only not yet – not yet. A moment more of striving, hesitation, suspense, that must become well-nigh intolerable in order to heighten the ultimate moment of joy. – Once more – a final tasting of this striving and yearning, this craving of the entire being, this last forcing of the will to deny oneself the fulfilment and the conclusion, in the knowledge that joy, when it comes, endures only for a moment . . . At last, at last joy could no longer be denied. It came, it poured over him: he resisted no more. His muscles relaxed, his head sank weakly on his shoulders, his eyes closed . . .

Some ninety years have passed since *Buddenbrooks* was written, and its language is probably too ripe to be entirely palatable today. Yet its ripeness here is clearly analogical: it suggests just how close to a sexual climax is the artistic denial which Hanno puts himself through, in order to make the artistic fulfilment he eventually attains, or to which he eventually succumbs, so much the more compelling. And on the very next page his mother, from whom he has inherited his musicality, speaks contemptuously of inferior art as 'a sort of insipid optimism . . . an easy gratification of each unformed wish, prompt satisfaction before the will is even roused . . . It is like nothing else on earth. It is mere flabby idealism.'

*

In Freudian terminology the word 'resistance' has a pejorative meaning only. It is seen as a predictable but purely negative phenomenon; it stands in the way of the self-understanding the patient is seeking; the only positive service it can be said to perform is that of confirming the accuracy of the analyst's interpretation of what is really going on in the patient's mind. That his resistance might be an index of his integrity, a source of health within him, is not to be contemplated; nor is the idea that it might reveal something to the analyst about his own preoccupations. The traffic is all one-way.

But then, it has always seemed strange to me, or even comical, that Freud should have been so insistent in his writings that every dream, every joke, every slip of the tongue, every forgetful or purposive action perpetrated by the people whose cases he was discussing, could be made to reveal a meaning that was unknown to them; whereas his interpretations of those phenomena are to be taken entirely at face value. For his interpretations, as Freud never wearies of proclaiming, are *true*: they have to be considered so because they are scientific – that being, to his mind, the flattest, most objective, least contestable variety of truth available. And the more myth-like and fantastic became his machinery for generating interpretations, the more he insisted that any view of them other than his own be dismissed, inevitably, as mere 'resistance'.

What that claim actually revealed (if I may offer my own interpretation of it) was the depth of his determination to escape from the mire of subjectivity which otherwise seemed to threaten him; which threatens us all whenever we venture on our interpretations of each other's words and behaviour, in books and out of them. It might be said, though, that a better way for us to achieve that end would be to welcome rather than to dismiss the resistances which people (and books) offer to the constructions we put on them. You want to know what the world might look like if you were not you? Then listen to what the other man says; or go away and read a book. (One by Freud, if you like.) In doing so you will discover soon enough, if the book is worth bothering with at all, or the man is worth listening to, that they both show a hunger quite as great as your own to escape from *their* subjectivity. Inevitably, any escape they succeed in making (with your help) is as fragile and provisional as the one you succeed in making (with their help); it has to be (for both sides); if it were not it would turn into another form of imprisonment. It can be disrupted at any moment and is bound to be forgotten, in some sense, like most other experiences, once it is over. But the fact that it can only arise through being shared should be seen as the sign that it is genuine, and not, as some people seem to suppose, that it is negligible. Moreover, as far as a book is concerned, the escape from the subjective mire that it offers us can be shared not only with its author, but also with its other readers.

There is obviously nothing certain or final or easily negotiable about the precarious release from the self thus attained; but, the assertions of some latterday literary theorists notwithstanding, there is also nothing random or hopeless about it.

PART TWO

BYRONIC

FOUR

WHAT'S EATING LARA?
(or Lord Byron's Guiltiest Secret)

The heroes of Byron's narrative poems are easy enough to describe. They are pale, proud, solitary; irresistible to women and yet indifferent to them; contemptuous of the world's opinions and rewards and yet filled with a jealous sense of honour; all are given to deadly laughs and withering frowns. In these respects they resemble closely enough their forebears in the Gothic novels of the eighteenth century; not to mention their innumerable successors in high and low fictions ever since. However, one further characteristic of the Byronic hero to which I want to pay attention here is always presented in the poems as somehow anterior to the others just mentioned; indeed, as their condition or cause. These heroes all carry in their breasts a secret of a terrible and tormenting kind. They are all haunted or cursed by memories which will give them no rest.

Thus the eponymous hero of *Lara*, who is described by Mario Praz in *The Romantic Agony* as 'the sombre portrait of [Byron's] idealised self':

> There was in him a vital scorn of all:
> As if the worst had fall'n which could befall,
> He stood a stranger in this breathing world
> An erring spirit from another hurled;
> A thing of dark imaginings, that shaped
> By choice the perils he by chance escaped;
> But 'scaped in vain, for in their memory yet
> His mind would half exult and half regret.

A contemporary follower of Byron's work would have recognised this guilt-laden stranger immediately. He had appeared fully fledged, already nourishing his hidden past, in the first Canto of *Childe Harold's Pilgrimage*, which was written before Byron became first the darling and then the scandal of London society:

> Yet oft-times in his maddest, mirthful mood
> Strange pangs would flash along Childe Harold's brow

31

As if the memory of some deadly feud
Or disappointed passion lurked below:
But this none knew, nor haply cared to know;
For his was not that open, artless soul
That feels relief by bidding sorrow flow.
Nor sought he friend to counsel or condole,
Whate'er this grief mote be, which he could not control.

The same character, with much the same affliction, appears in *The Giaour* – metamorphosed first into a symbolic Scorpion:

The Mind that broods o'er guilty woes,
  Is like the Scorpion girt by fire;
In circle narrowing as it glows,
The flames around their captive close,
Till inly searched by thousand throes,
  And maddening in her ire,
One sad and sole relief she knows,
The sting she nourished for her foes,
Whose venom never yet was vain,
Gives but one pang and cures all pain . . .

and then into a penitential Friar:

Dark and unearthly is the scowl
That glares beneath his cowl.
The flash of that dilating eye
Reveals too much of times gone by;
Though varying, indistinct its hue,
Oft will his glance the gazer rue.

. . .

And there are hues not always faded,
Which speak a mind not all degraded
Even by the crimes through which it waded:
The common crowd but see the gloom
Of wayward deeds, and fitting doom.

And as for the Corsair of *The Corsair* – what can one say about him but ditto, ditto, ditto?

Though smooth his voice and calm his general mien,
Still seems there something he would not have seen:

His features' deepening lines and varying hue
At times attracted, yet perplex'd the view.
As if within that murkiness of mind
Work'd feelings fearful, and yet undefined;
Such might it be – that none could truly tell –
Too close inquiry his glance would sternly quell.

The intention to provoke the reader's curiosity is plain enough. However, any reader who obediently goes through the poems in the hope of finding what actually happened in the past to cause these dreadful frowns and stings and convulsions of remorse will soon find that his efforts have been wasted. All the poems purport to be narratives of some kind (the rhapsodic *Childe Harold* included); but even when their plots apparently turn wholly on the hero's hidden secret at last being divulged, it remains a secret still. Indeed, what the reader becomes aware of is a kind of panic within the poem whenever the exigencies of its plot threaten to force a revelation from it.

This is certainly the case with *Lara*, which I shall use as my prime example. Lavishly equipped with the usual Gothic fixtures and fittings, the tale includes various murders, a civil war, a country laid waste, the discovery that Lara's faithful boy-companion is really a woman in disguise, and many other such excitements. The central episode in the drama, the one which actually triggers off the dire consequences just alluded to, takes place when the lordly Lara, on returning home after a long spell abroad, goes to a party given by a neighbour. At the party he is challenged about his past by a stranger (never identified in the course of the poem) who recognises him from some previous occasion and says to him, after many meaningful stares and a few challenging words, 'Art thou not that lord whose deeds – ?' At that point Lara interrupts him; he does not allow the stranger to finish the question; as a result they instantly arrange to have a duel. Various catastrophes follow immediately; the rest later. Now that dash (' – ') after the word 'deeds' is all we ever learn about Lara's past. Instead of facts we are offered, quite literally, only punctuation. A dash and a question mark.

Much the same is true of the other poems I have mentioned. The Corsair is a pirate chief; but Byron is at pains to tell us that he does not feel the remorse which stings him from time to time *because* he is a pirate. That would be much too banal. No, this Corsair became a pirate because of the usual, unnameable, unmentionable, terrible something in the past which drove him further into a life of crime –

Yet was not Conrad thus by Nature sent
To lead the guilty – guilt's worst instrument –
His soul was changed, before his deeds had driven
Him forth to war with men and forfeit heaven.

When we turn to the Giaour – he of the cowl and the scowl – we discover that the only specified crime he commits in the course of the poem is to kill the Tartar chieftain who had put his (the Giaour's) loved one in a sack and dumped her in the river: *not* a crime, one might think, which warrants the years he subsequently spends in a savagely penitential state of mind.

So at the heart of these poems there appears to be a mystery. Or rather, a double mystery. There is the one which Byron tries to create within each poem through his hints and whispers and punctuation, his excited gestures and horrified yet exultant exclamations, about the events or series of events which are supposed to lie behind the action. What are the crimes we are to assume these heroes are really guilty of? That is the first problem. The second problem is: what is Byron himself up to? What is he trying to hide and reveal by pursuing his heroes so pertinaciously with these accusations?

*

To turn for answers to these questions to what is known about the many lurid passages in Byron's life – its ruinous love affairs and episodes of incest, homosexuality, debauchery, debt, and the rest – is to fall precisely into the trap Byron himself has laid for us. It is to allow him wholly to determine how his poems should be read. Listen to the tortuous syntax of confession and retraction, asseveration and denial, revelation and concealment, in the following paragraph from the dedication to *The Corsair*:

> With regard to my story, and stories in general, I should have been glad to have rendered my personages more amiable, if possible, inasmuch as I have sometimes been criticised, and considered no less responsible for their deeds and qualities than if all had been personal. Be it so – if I have ever deviated into the gloomy vanity of 'drawing from self', the pictures are probably like, since they are unfavourable; and if not, those who know me are undeceived, and those who do not, I have little interest in undeceiving. I have no particular desire that any but acquaintances should think the author better than the beings of his imagining; but I cannot help a little surprise, and perhaps amusement, at some odd critical exceptions in the present instance, when I see several bards (far more deserving I allow) in very reputable plight, and quite exempted from all participation in the faults of those heroes, who, nevertheless might be found with little more morality than 'The Giaour' and perhaps – but no – I must admit Childe Harold to be a very repulsive personage; and as to his identity, those who like it must give him whatever 'alias' they please.

Yes, he insists on our identifying him with his hero, even as he scorns us for attempting to make such an identification; yes, he wants our awed and prurient speculation to move endlessly from poem to author and from author back to poem, so that each might in turn intensify (even as it seems to resolve) the mystery which the other presents to us. To this end everything serves: the phantasmagoric narratives of the poems, their gliding, resistless rhythms and rhymes, the pre-emptive strikes they try to make against the reader's mirth or scepticism. (See for example the warnings, issued in almost identical language each time, against our looking too closely at the poems' chief characters: 'Oft will his glance the gazer rue' we are told about the Giaour; and about the Corsair, 'Too close inquiry his glance would sternly quell.' Exactly!) Like any other bad writer, Byron is trying to get what he can out of the reader (amazement, fear, admiration) on tick, as it were – without delivering the goods. Or if they are to be delivered, this will be done outside the poem, in life, in the world of rumour and gossip: his looks will have to do, his lineage, his love affairs, his club-foot, even (it might be said) his manner of going to his death.

Given his reliance on the life to sustain and deepen the mystery of the poems, and on the poems to sustain and deepen the mystery of the life, it is perhaps not so surprising that Byron is the only English poet whose name has been turned into an abstract noun: Byronism. Adjectives made out of writers' names abound in the language (Shakespearean, Dickensian, Eliotic etc). But to have named after oneself a demeanour, a habit of mind and feeling, a cultural condition, and to have it recognised and imitated all over Europe and beyond, not just in one's own lifetime but for a century and more afterwards, is a unique achievement. It is not surprising, too, in the light of what has just been said about the poems, that a sense of hollowness and imposture should be a central element of the various forms which Byronism took. True, there are passages in *Childe Harold*, and more flickeringly in the other poems, which are powerful and effective enough, poetically speaking, to make time work for them rather than against them (to adapt the phrase Coleridge used about Wordsworth's verse). But let the 'badness' of the Byron poems be given its due. It may make them seem grotesquely dated to our tastes, but without it, without all that was faked and empty in them, they would never have been able to take hold as they did of the contemporary imagination.

It is not just that the readers of Byron's age, like readers today, enjoyed trash; and the more portentous it was, the more fluent, the more titillatingly knowledgeable about evil, the more 'literary' in certain obvious ways, the more they admired it. (Again, just like readers today – though the styles of vulgarity and bad faith we respond to are different.) There is another and more interesting sense in which one can say that the hollowness of the poems helped to account for their success. What made them so effective in reaching into the minds of their readers is that they are *about* hollowness, they are about bad faith and insincerity. Indeed, one can go further and say that the central, tormenting secret which the heroes of the poems (and their creator) try to guard so jealously from prying eyes is their own suspicion that they are fakers.

*

F.R. Leavis once wrote that every major work of literature forces us to define anew what we mean by sincerity. As it happens, this could also be said about every mediocre work of literature, every television soap opera, the speech of every politician canvassing for our votes. (After all, the politician sincerely wants our votes; he might also sincerely want to feel what he claims he feels on our behalf.) Sincerity is never a stable characteristic or quality of the personality; it is rather a kind of balancing act within the self; an equipoise which, as various writers have remarked, enables us to think (or know) what we feel, and at the same time to feel (or believe) what we know. Even this kind of definition is ultimately inadequate, however, in apparently not allowing for the possibility of our being aware that just such an equipoise might be quite beyond our capacities: when what we know on the one hand and feel on the other, when what we tell ourselves and what we actually believe, are at such odds with one another it is difficult for us to imagine a reconciliation between them.

In other words, while a person may wish to be sincere, the state of 'being sincere' is not really subject to his will. To will oneself to be sincere is (almost by definition) not to be sincere. For the will turns out to be just one of the elements within the personality as a whole which have to be in balance with one another if the state is to be attained; and the will itself cannot will that balance into being. In these respects sincerity resembles certain other states of being or modes of feeling highly prized by the Romantics: 'spontaneity' for example, or 'joy', or even 'creativity'. The paradox of these, especially when they are elevated into something resembling ideals of behaviour, is that the more tensely the will is directed towards them, the more certain they are to elude it.

Byron's narrative poems provide us with a striking illustration of the workings of this paradoxical form of self-bafflement and self-betrayal.* Never to feel wholly what you wish to feel – and to wish it all the more intensely for that very reason; never to be able to believe in the veracity of whatever feelings you do have – and to make threatening gestures towards anyone who has his own doubts about them; to be aware of a sickening gap between assertion and inner state every time you open your mouth – not least when you open your mouth precisely to deny that there is such a gap . . . whether or not it is a crime to feel the 'throes' and 'pangs' of that kind of insincerity I do not know. That it can be a torment is certain: more of a torment than the remorse and evil, criminality and isolation, which are the ostensible subject of this particular group of poems. Especially when we may suspect that the poet knew not only the 'gloomy vanity' of having 'drawn' his heroes 'from self', as he put it, but the even gloomier vanity of knowing that he is now obliged – for sincerity's sake! – to draw his own self from *them*.

*

* D.H. Lawrence's *Women in Love*, I suggest below, provides us with yet another form of it.

Perhaps the greatest of all literary gifts is the capacity of the writer to turn the misgivings and weaknesses which corrode or sometimes even destroy him as a man into a source of strength and vitality in his work. The ability to invert or transvalue weakness in this way is always a disconcerting one, even to those who possess it; it is not surprising that our conventional pieties about art, and about what it can do for us, have so little to say on the topic. In Byron's case – and one can do no more than guess that it could have taken place only after the break-up of his marriage, after his disgrace, after his expulsion from polite society and hurried departure for Europe: in short, after he had shown to everybody's satisfaction, his own included, that he was 'worthy' of his heroes – this capacity was demonstrated in striking fashion. His narrative poems, with that fixed, demonic scowl on their foreheads, were the literary record of his attempt to overcome by an effort of will what I have called the torment of insincerity which had always haunted him. Every clenched denial and fierce assertion in those poems, every dark hint at what had better be left unspoken, had been intended to silence not only the doubters and deriders without – though on the whole they had shown themselves only too eager to be convinced – but the many sceptical voices within.

But if he attended to those voices, and even gave them tongue; if his will unclenched itself and he 'accepted' his own insincerity, instead of trying so hard to deny it – what then? If he acknowledged that none of his gestures and postures could be relied on, that his most impassioned and alarming utterances had always teetered on the very edge of absurdity, that he was a faker, a chancer, a man uncertain of himself, one unable to sustain his own belief in whatever he claimed he believed or would have liked to believe – what would happen? What would the effect be?

I am not suggesting, of course, that Byron asked himself questions in these terms, or anything like them. As far as the reader is concerned, the source of such questions, as well as the complicated answers to them, are to be found in *Don Juan*: a comic masterpiece whose very principle as a poem is that nothing which the narrator says is to be trusted for a moment. His tongue is always in his cheek. Every attitude he adopts in the poem is provisional: he will abandon it in an instant for the sake of a laugh, a good rhyme, a piece of insolent moralising, an outburst of perfunctory passion. He lures us on with sighs of longing and exclamations of defiance; then he trips us into a pit of bathos; then he looks down over the rim of the pit and sympathises with our plight. He will change mood in mid-line, if it pleases him; or he will save up such a change until the last couplet of a stanza, and then do it all the more violently for the momentary restraint he has seemed to show; or he will maintain a single elevated tone for stanza after stanza, only to let it go quite casually and indifferently in the end, as if neither humour nor seriousness were his business, but ours, plodding on behind him. Sometimes he is frank, confident, engaging; sometimes aristocratically haughty or fatigued; sometimes smutty in schoolboyish fashion; always whatever he feels like being just at that particular moment.

One consequence of all this is that many of the dramatic and pathetic effects which Byron strove for in his more serious poems actually come off more successfully in *Don Juan* than elsewhere. This is a measure of how much he had managed to liberate himself from the obligations and constrictions of the past. I am thinking of episodes like the love affair between Don Juan and Haidée in Canto Two of the poem. Young, unspoiled love, full of innocence and passion, and soon to be destroyed by a brutal world, had always been one of Byron's favourite themes. One of his most embarrassing, too. Here, because he is jocular about so much around and within the relationship, he is also able to be convincing and touching in his description of the lovers' passion. Much the same is true, though there he is dealing with scenes of carnage and confusion, of the famous battle described in Canto Eight.

But perhaps the greatest compliment one can pay to *Don Juan* is to say that it is manifestly written by the author of the letters: which is far from the case with the earlier narratives. A few exceptions aside, not all of them satirical, it is extremely difficult to reconcile the author of the letters – so full of irreverence, shrewdness, harshness, curiosity about the behaviour of others and candour about his own – with the author of the earlier poems; and almost impossible to do so with the simplifying scowler and braggart of the narratives. But in *Don Juan* the reconciliation is complete; or rather, there is no need to make a reconciliation. The whole man is there in the poem, just as he is in the letters. Nothing need be held back or sent away as unsuitable for his purposes: no reflection, or appetite, or self-revelation. They are all entitled to their say. They all find it in the poem.

In Canto Three of *Don Juan* a poet appears at a party given by Juan and Haidée, and sings 'The Isles of Greece'. Then Byron comments on the performance as only he – who knew so much about the lies that poets tell about their feelings, and the truth they are compelled to tell about their lies, and the effects of both on others – had earned the right to:

> His strain display'd some feeling – right or wrong;
>   And feeling, in a poet, is the source
> Of others' feeling; but they are such liars,
> And take all colours – like the hands of dyers.
>
> But words are things, and a small drop of ink,
>   Falling like dew, upon a thought, produces
> That which makes thousands, perhaps millions, think;
>   'Tis strange, the shortest letter which man uses
> Instead of speech, may form a lasting link
>   Of ages; to what straits old Time reduces
> Frail man, when paper – even a rag like this,
> Survives himself, his tomb, and all that's his!

What's Eating Lara?

And when his bones are dust, his grave a blank,
   His station, generation, even his nation,
Become a thing, or nothing, save to rank
   In chronological commemoration,
Some dull MS. oblivion long has sank,
   Or graven stone found in a barrack's station
In digging the foundation of a closet,
May turn his name up, as a rare deposit.

FIVE

JEW D'ESPRIT

If you want to get ahead in the world, you cannot afford to be contemptuous of or ironic about your own fantasies. It is indeed important to be able, as Wordsworth puts it, to part

> Vague longing that is bred by want of power
> From paramount impulse not to be withstood.

Yet the poet's phrasing implicitly suggests that what finally matters is not so much what we long for, but the intensity and the confidence with which we long for it, and the place our longings assume in our deepest conceptions of ourselves.

In these respects, all ambitious people are probably much alike. However, an imaginative writer who nourishes the hope of achieving great worldly success would appear to have one important advantage over others. By incorporating aspects of his ambition in his work, and elaborating on it in poems, or plays, or stories, he enables his readers to participate in his fantasies of power and eminence. If he is talented enough, or just lucky enough, they will then reward him for doing so by heaping fame and fortune on him in the 'real' world, the world outside his books. When Disraeli, at the age of twenty-six, published his third novel, which was promisingly entitled *The Young Duke*, his father is reputed to have asked: 'What does Ben know of dukes?' The vacuities and turgidities of the novel reveal that in one sense the author knew nothing about them. In another sense, the novel reveals that what he knew about dukes was what mattered most to him: namely, that he wanted to spend as much of his life as he could in their company.

The extent to which he succeeded remains astonishing to contemplate, given the race and class into which he was born. The cabinets which he was to lead abounded in dukes and the scions of ducal families. Ironically, however, he achieved this success by being even bolder in life than he ever dared to be in his fictions – something which can be said about very few novelists indeed. Not that he was timid, as a writer, in tackling a wide variety of themes. He wrote about London high life, as if from within, when he was hardly anything more than a solicitor's upstart clerk; he produced fiction about German court life, religious revivals in the Middle East, the relations between Byron and Shelley, the machinations of Catholic prelates against an upright Englishman (a duke, inevitably), and Garibaldi's march on Rome; as well as the politics of Young England and the 'Condition-of-England Question'; not to mention a verse epic on the French revolution.

Yet for all the variety of his fictions, and for all the sketchy bravado of their comic and satiric thrusts (for which it seems to me they have been excessively praised), many of the books can leave one with a rather surprising impression of caution and uncertainty. They seem to be weakened by a lack of drive, a fear of giving offence, which is revealed most strikingly, perhaps, in the absence of villains within them: something I have never seen remarked on in those critical discussions of the novels which I have read. It is as if the author, who was to become notorious as a mature politician for his unparalleled powers of vituperation, did not wish to make enemies through his fictions: certainly not by enabling any of his readers to see themselves mirrored in his pages as this or that outright evildoer. The books do contain some thinly persuasive toadies, buffoons, schemers and overbearing nobs; but almost everyone in them lives in a splendid house, looks lovely, and is ultimately well disposed to everyone else. The effect, on this reader anyway, is extraordinarily dispiriting. Even *Sybil*, the novel which is ostensibly devoted to the plight of the poor, and which features both the urban and rural proletariats in some unusually lively postures of menace and pathos, ends with the poverty-stricken heroine becoming in her own right, and to general applause, an heiress of great title and broad acres, as well as the spouse of the Earl of Marney.

How different all these quasi-idylls are from the story of his own life, with its debts and shady business deals, dubious love affairs, scroungings for patronage, early and obscure breakdowns, humiliations endured and revenges taken; its unbounded audacity and calculated displays of aggression; its ever-vigilant opportunism and its deep, half-conscious, unyielding prepossessions and drives. 'I wish to act what I write,' he confided in a diary he kept as a young man, when the gap between action and written word was perhaps at its widest. What he actually went on to produce, for the most part, was a series of benignly aristocratic reveries, seasoned with half-baked but (to him) indispensable theorisings about race, religion, and the 'traditionary' strengths of the crown and the landed classes. Of these latter elements in his fiction more will be said shortly. But we can be sure that had he reversed the order of his verbs, and written what he had acted – as his model and idol, Lord Byron, was rightly or wrongly believed to have done – he would never have become Prime Minister, the Earl of Beaconsfield, and confidant of the Queen.

Byron had spoken at length and yet cryptically, in poem after poem, of the histrionic self-doubt and sense of evil which, he wished his readers to suppose, had goaded him from one extravagant action to another; he had then moved on to the wonderfully truth-revealing irresponsibility and mischief of *Don Juan*. The result? A European-wide reputation, and one great poem, certainly; but also disgrace, exile, death at an early age on a remote Greek peninsula. Whereas this is how Robert Blake, in his celebrated biography, *Disraeli*, describes his subject during his second term as Prime Minister:

> [He] attended the dinners and receptions of the beaumonde with the assiduity of a man half his age . . . He was not only at the top of the political pyramid, he was very close to the top of the social pyramid, too. He was sought by every great hostess. He knew exactly who was who in that restricted world, their incomes, their love-affairs, their past or impending scandals . . . It is odd to think of this gaunt wheezing figure, the pallor of his lined face accentuated rather than relieved by the rouge which, like Palmerston in old age, he regularly applied, dining night after night during the season amidst the glitter of the great London houses, listening impassively to the gay-rattle of duchesses and the social gossip of men-about-town.

Now the gap between word and act mentioned earlier was well and truly closed: jammed tight, indeed.

*

In *Disraeli's Grand Tour: Benjamin Disraeli and the Holy Land 1830–31* Robert Blake concentrates on one colourful episode, or sequence of episodes, in the young Disraeli's life: the tour through the Mediterranean and Near East which he undertook with the man who was intended to become his brother-in-law. On the way they were joined by a raffish Wykhamist by the name of James Clay, a friend of Disraeli's brother, and also by Tita Falcieri, who had formerly been a servant to Byron. Indeed, though Robert Blake does not write of it in these terms, much of the tour might almost be considered a Byronic pilgrimage of a kind. Not only did Disraeli acquire the services of Tita as a result of it, but he actually followed the poet's footsteps in going successively to Spain, Malta, Albania and Greece. This must surely have been a conscious undertaking on his part. (It should be remembered that his admiration for Byron was little short of a hereditary trait. His father, 'a learned Jew' as Byron described him, had been an acquaintance of the poet and an infatuated critic of his work.) Like Byron, he wrote vivid letters home, which dwell on the exotic, and dismiss it; like Byron, he dressed himself up in Turkish costume, and consorted with the local chieftains and their followers; from Clay's letters it would seem that, like Byron again, though probably in a less elaborate fashion, he took advantage of the sexual opportunities which came his way in the course of his journeyings. Unfortunately the whole adventure ended badly for the young men: Meredith, the brother-in-law-to-be, contracted smallpox in Cairo, and died of it within a few days. Disraeli then returned as rapidly as he could to England, and to his grief-stricken sister. His first real entry into London society (where for a time he was known as the 'Jew d'esprit') still lay some months ahead.

In one important respect the route of his travels in the Levant had differed from Byron's. He and Clay, though not Meredith, had entered the Holy Land and made the ascent to Jerusalem; they had spent the months from January to March 1831 on this section of their journey. No less than four of Disraeli's novels, *Contarini Fleming, Alroy, Tancred* and *Lothair*, were to bear the marks of this experience. One of them, *Alroy*, is probably the worst he ever wrote (which is saying something); the others, in different ways and in different degrees, are not much good either. English literature can be said charitably, therefore, to have gained only a series of oddities from the pilgrimage. And Disraeli himself? Robert Blake suggests that his travels in the provinces of the Ottoman Empire inclined him, when he was in office many years later, to take a more favourable attitude to Turkish power than was common among Englishmen of his time. However, the author is more interested in tracing the effects of the visit to the Holy Land on Disraeli's view of his own position as a Jew converted to Christianity and an aspirant man-of-letters and politician. Did it make some sort of (premature) Zionist out of him? Did it enable him to develop that conviction of his belonging to a grand 'Arabian' or 'Asian' aristocracy – 'of unmixed blood', as he put it in *Coningsby* – which was to be a source of strength to him in his dealings with the English grandees among whom he made his career? Did it encourage him to conjure out of some recess of his mind the notion of 'theocratic equality'? (This I take to be a stab at reconciling Judaism with Christianity, as well as a way of reconciling his sense of the importance of religion in the life of nations with a consciousness of his own incapacity for genuine or personally felt religious emotion.)

The answer to all these questions must be a qualified yes: qualified not only because they are difficult questions, but also because everything Disraeli said or did is subject to qualification by something else he may have done or said at some other time. Consider, for instance, the idea of Disraeli as a kind of Zionist-before-Zionism. Surely, one thinks, his novel *Alroy*, which is about a medieval Jewish leader who wishes to redeem the Jews from captivity and bring them back to Zion – a novel which Disraeli himself spoke of as an expression of his 'ideal ambition' – should provide us with irrefutable, positive evidence on that score. Well, it does not. We are not long into the novel before we find that the hero is bored with the Jews and Zion and what they have to offer him. 'Shall this quick blaze of empire,' he asks in characteristic vein, 'sink to a glimmering and a twilight sway over some petty province? ... I have no mandate to yield my glorious empire for my meanest province.' So much for the Holy Land! Admittedly, Alroy is chastised in the novel for these Tamurlane-like vauntings. But we have only to recall his creator's attitude to the British Empire and its Queen to know that he would never have exchanged the position he eventually achieved, or even the prospect of gaining it, in order to become what his Alroy scornfully describes as 'the decent patriarch of a pastoral horde'. So much for the Chosen People and their wonderfully undiluted blood!*

Though Disraeli refers bitterly in several of his novels, and elsewhere, to the sufferings of the Jews at the hands of Christians and Moslems, it is noteworthy that he can never really bring himself to portray in his fiction a suffering or disadvantaged Jew. Pride, shame, and that most potent of emotions which is composed indistinguishably of both, would never permit him to do so. (It is doubtful, according to Robert Blake, whether during his stay in Jerusalem he even visited the Jewish quarter of the city, where he would have been unable to avoid seeing plenty of disadvantaged members of his race.) Instead, virtually all the Jewish characters in his novels are rich, haughty, powerful, beautiful, wise, and (most implausible of all, and most unlike Disraeli's own experience of the world) wholeheartedly admired by the people among whom they live. The greatest of these paragons is the financier and traveller, Sidonia, in *Coningsby, Sybil* and *Tancred*, who owns everything, knows everybody, and describes the power and pre-eminence of the Jews in terms that could not be outdone by the most luridly paranoiac fantasies of a convinced anti-Semite. In fact, with his restlessness, his lordly airs, his mysterious comings and goings, and the secret sorrow or crime (his Jewishness) which in some sense cuts him off from ordinary intercourse with society, Sidonia represents a curious cultural transmutation of the Byronic hero. As it were: from Childe Harold to Rothschild, in a single generation.

Here and elsewhere Disraeli was using his peculiar notions about the Jews and their role in history as a mode of self-advancement; or, to put the same point in another but equally meaningful way, his self-advancement demanded that something special and striking be made of his Jewish origins and appearance. One can make a similar kind of observation about his espousal (after some divagations) of the Tory cause in general, and of the cause of Young England in particular. (In *Disraeli* Robert Blake characterises Young England as 'the Oxford Movement translated by Cambridge from religion into politics'.) Only the Tories, only a party which supported the prerogatives of the crown, the privileges of the peers, and the rights of the Established Church, could have tolerated or afforded so exotic a personage as its spokesman and leader. Disraeli knew this better, and sooner, than the Tories themselves did; and he acted, and wrote, and theorised accordingly. He was a subtle and passionate man, with an indomitable will and a mind that kept its alertness and flexibility to the very end. (He published *Endymion*, which seems to me his most entertaining novel, or at any rate his least embarrassing novel, at the age of seventy-six, after his second term as Prime

---

* 'Mosaic Arab' is the preposterous term he invents for them in *Coningsby*. Anything rather than the three-letter word, Jew. Four years later, in *Dombey and Son*, Dickens snapped up the phrase – and applied it to a second-hand furniture dealer.

Minister.) But all these advantages would have availed him little if he had not also had the capacity to fabricate histories and ideologies which in effect served as self-justificatory myths in his strivings with himself and others. Paradoxically enough, these myths, which purported to describe and explain what had actually happened in the world, or was going to happen in it, were by far the most important fictions he ever invented; and he did not merely act on them, as he had asked of himself in his diary. He did more. He very nearly came to believe in them.

*

I say 'very nearly' not only because of the general caution issued earlier about Disraeli's attitudes and beliefs, but because one of the most unexpected features of his writings is that he seems to have valued the myths presented in them precisely *as* myths. Indeed, it would appear that that was how he wanted his readers and ultimately the people of England to value them too. They would be all the more welcome, he hoped, since they would sound so unlike everything else that passed for political discourse in England. Or so his tone of earnest yet sardonic advocacy suggests. When (echoing or anticipating the famous distinction in German sociological thought between *Gemeinschaft* and *Gesellschaft*) he lamented the decline of English society from the 'community' it once had been to the 'aggregation' it had subsequently become, and blamed for this sad development such forces as Whiggery, capitalism, Dissent, the rise of a rapacious middle class and the collapse of the self-confidence of the aristocracy – when he did all this he seems to have been enunciating a heroic fantasy which he wanted others to recognise as such. What is more, through the mouth of his own Sidonia in *Coningsby* he acknowledged a tendency towards myth-making of this kind to be a mark of the outsider, of the man who lacks what Sidonia calls 'the strong reality of existence' which should come naturally to the citizen of a free country.

In these respects, paradoxes and all, Disraeli strikingly resembles two other canonical figures in English intellectual conservative history, Edmund Burke and T.S. Eliot. They too were outsiders, from Ireland in the one case and from the United States in the other; they too wrote, as Disraeli did, with a propagandistic intensity of the organic or hereditary bonds which, they believed, alone could preserve society against the depredations of shallow ideology and rapid material change. With all three of them, again, a peculiar contradiction is to be observed between what their work says about others (and society in general) and what it reveals directly and indirectly about themselves.

The conservative frame of mind, by definition, has a strong regard for the power of what is given and indefeasible in human nature and circumstance, as well as in existing institutions and arrangements. In their writings these men expressed their regard, or veneration, for a 'traditionary' order with all the force of which they were capable; they expressed, too, the pessimism and suspicion of change which inevitably accompanies it. However, those same writings of theirs, and the careers which the writings in effect created, show all three men to have been endowed with a high degree of personal ambition; and, going with it, a quite exceptional dissatisfaction with the circumstances of birth and background which fate had apparently allotted to *them*.

But then, who should feel more strongly than just such self-transformers a nostalgia for an organic, unbroken continuity with the past? And if, in the end, they were compelled to invent for their fellow-countrymen some or much of the past to which they declared themselves to be so attached – well, who was there who could do the job with more feeling?

*

There is one entertaining anecdote from Disraeli's Grand Tour which appears in Monypenny and Buckle's two-volume, official, Victorian biography, but which, rather surprisingly, Robert Blake does not include in his book. In a letter from Albania to his fiancée, Meredith wrote of a Greek doctor who gazed wonderingly at Disraeli's garb of red shirt, silver buttons, green pantaloons, jacket festooned with ribbons, and Turkish slippers – and then asked: *'Questo vestito Inglese o di fantasia?'* To this there came a reply which Monypenny describes as 'oracular', but which seems to me richly appropriate to the story as a whole: *'Inglese e fantastico.'*

SIX

THEODORE HERZL

◆

In its general outline the Herzl story or legend is well-known. Once upon a time there was a Viennese Jewish dandy and *littérateur* who had established a reputation as a gifted but rather frivolous playwright and journalist. As a correspondent for the famous Vienna daily, *Neue Freie Presse*, he was given the task of covering the Dreyfus trial in Paris. The anti-Semitic outbursts which the trial produced from every level of French society, supposedly the most enlightened in Europe, shocked him into a new awareness of his own Jewishness, which had hitherto meant little to him, and of the dangers which confronted the entire Jewish people. In this state of shock he hurriedly composed his most famous book, *The Jewish State: An Attempt at a Modern Solution of the Jewish Question*. Immediately afterwards he went on to create, almost single-handedly, a political movement dedicated to bringing into being the state which his book had proposed. A mere nine years later, at the age of forty-four, he was dead, having utterly exhausted himself in constant effort on behalf of his great cause. Initially he was derided as a madman and visionary both by the Jews he was trying to save and by the Gentiles whose support he tried to solicit. Today his portrait hangs in the chamber of the Israeli Parliament (the Knesset) in Jerusalem; on a hilltop nearby, which bears his name and which overlooks the city, his body lies enshrined.

By and large, this legend is accurate, as Amos Elon's compendious and absorbing biography, *Herzl*, reveals. The legend does contain some errors of fact (e.g. Herzl had become much preoccupied with 'the Jewish question' well before the Dreyfus trial began), and more errors of emphasis (e.g. the idea of political Zionism was not as dramatically novel, when Herzl proposed it, as the legend would suggest). Nevertheless, one of the virtues of Amos Elon's biography is that it demonstrates just how much unfamiliar and uncomfortable detail the legend is capable of incorporating without losing its shape. One reads the story, just as one reads much of Herzl's own writing, with a singular mixture of wonder and embarrassment; in the end it becomes difficult to tell the one emotion from the other.

Why embarrassment? Well, take the only son of a well-to-do Jewish family; admire him extravagantly, indulge his every whim, and prophesy constantly to him that some day he will be a great man; teach him virtually nothing about Judaism, Jewish history, or the Hebrew language; let him grow up moody, lonely, and 'poetic' in his aspirations; fill him with banal, enlightened notions about progress, science, and the universal brotherhood of man; encourage in him a multitude of snobberies, including a wholehearted contempt for commerce and a self-abasing admiration for all that is most 'aristocratic' and 'exclusive' in the culture and society around him; let him yearn from afar for blond, blue-eyed Gentile girls; inculcate in him a sentimental attachment to the history and language of the country he lives in; and finally, curse him with ambitions that far outstrip his talents . . . and what have you got? The father of a nation? Or any one of half-a-dozen people you might have known at university?

Of course, these familiar characteristics and tendencies took the coloration of their time and place, the Vienna and Paris of the 1880s and 1890s, and expressed themselves accordingly. As a student Herzl did everything that was to be expected of him. He joined a students' duelling club and was struck about the face with a sabre in traditional style. He composed fervent pan-German nationalist hymns. He patronised *grisettes* and got a dose of the clap. He wrote plays which he submitted for production in the Viennese theatres. He considered committing suicide, at some length. In copious notes, diaries, letters, and essays, which are both excruciatingly self-conscious and childishly self-betraying, he solemnly recorded his reflections and impulses, as befitted the important writer he intended to become. 'Although,' wrote the Budapest-born youngster to his parents, who were then living in Vienna, 'there are many Viennese and Budapest Jews here [in a holiday resort] the rest of the vacationing population is very pleasant'. In loftier, more Byronic mood, perhaps even admitting Viennese and Budapest Jews within his conspectus, he confided to his diary, 'Nothing on earth, or very little, deserves our wrath. With disdain and pity it is possible . . . to get on very well in the world.' Or, 'At the sound of music, sweet intoxicating dreams of future fame and glory envelop my drunken heart.' Or, 'I do not carry a great work within me. Break your pen, poor devil!' Or, simply, 'To be blond is everything.'

Such posturings and schemings, vanities and predictable torments, cannot be separated from what might be thought of as the deeper strains and compulsions of his nature, or from his response to the griefs and disappointments life inflicted upon him. Towards the end of his adolescence his only sister, whom he adored, died suddenly of typhoid fever; some years later he wrote a passage of sardonic self-analysis, almost worthy of Dickens's David Copperfield or Pip, of how he had behaved at the time. His devotion to his parents, always intense, became positively sickly after his sister's death. His enduring isolation from his contemporaries was a fact as well as a pose. The striking success he enjoyed as a journalist, and the far more modest degree of recognition he achieved as a playwright, did not assuage his feeling that he had failed to justify his literary ambitions. In his late twenties, he married a wealthy, pretty, and hopelessly unstable girl; thereupon the marriage promptly turned bad and became a source of constant misery to him. His melancholy, which had once been almost soothing, a proof of the refinement of his sensibility ('I can only be happy when I am absolutely miserable'), settled into a real affliction. Even his vanity about his personal appearance had its oddly sombre or significant aspects.

The last point is worth dwelling on, if only because it shows how inextricably confused in Herzl's case (as they are in so many others) were those 'accidental' or 'trivial' circumstances which one would not ordinarily imagine to be linked to the birth of major political and ideological movements. Would Herzl have become a Zionist if he had been as 'blond' as he obviously wished to be? I greatly doubt it. Consider the difficulty of his position. On the one hand he was (and he was proud to be) a man of the most striking appearance. Tall, handsome, upright, dignified in his bearing, he was noticed at once in any group in which he found himself. However, the looks which drew so much attention to him were as far from his own ideal of pure, blond Teutonic knighthood as it would be possible to imagine. His complexion was olive, his hair and beard were black, his nose was large, his eyes were dark and deep. He looked like a prince, indeed: a Prince of Judah. Or perhaps of Assyria. (In the later pictures, including the one hanging in the Knesset building, his resemblance to a figure from ancient Assyrian statuary is quite remarkable.) So what was he to do, given his preoccupation with his appearance? Forego the special destiny it seemed to have marked out for him? Or find some unprecedented way of fulfilling it?

*

The painful and intricate relationship between certain forms of Jewish self-hatred and Zionism has never perhaps been more clearly demonstrated than in the life of the founder of the movement. This is not to suggest that all the bafflements and blockages suffered by Herzl were a direct consequence of his position as a Jew. Still less is it to belittle his all-too accurate perception of the catastrophic situation in which European Jewry would sooner or later find itself. If he was driven, around the time of the Dreyfus trial, to try to reconstruct imaginatively the future of an entire people, it was because the tensions and contradictions within him – between the man he was and the writer he wished to be; and the man he wished to be and the writer he was – had become as intolerable as the provocations of history; and because he had reached a point where he could no longer make a distinction between his injured self and the injuries suffered by the group to which, willy-nilly, he belonged.

In a matter of weeks – weeks of sleeplessness, scribblings, loneliness, opera-going, incoherent wanderings through the streets and parks of Paris – Herzl was swept away by his sudden vision of the Jewish people sovereign once again in a country of its own. (The operas he went to were those of Wagner: of course, one is tempted to add.) During that period of exaltation he transformed himself irrevocably from a hurt and haughty man of letters into the would-be Moses of his people. It was a transformation that was eventually to cost him everything: family, fortune, life. 'I think,' he wrote in the diary he began at this time, 'for me life has ended and world-history has begun . . . At night it burns within me when my eyes are closed; I cannot hide from it.'

From that point onwards, it might be supposed, the reader of his biography should begin to feel wonder and admiration only, tinged perhaps with pity. But embarrassment persists too. The transformations of an individual's intellectual and emotional capacities likely to be brought about by religious conversions, obsessions, manias, madness, even drug trances, are more limited than we often wish to suppose. (Some of what is written on such subjects reminds one of those old comic-book advertisements: 'I was a 90lb emotional and intellectual weakling until I discovered . . . MADNESS!') To compare Herzl's seizure by the Zionist idea with an attack of madness is of course unfair to him. But it is equally unfair to expect him somehow to have been able to step forward new-born out of the shell of himself. The astonishing energies that were released as a result of his discovery of the Zionist cause had to make do with the equipment, mentally and morally speaking, which had always been his; he simply had no other.

Thus his determination to find a solution to 'the Jewish question' had been heralded by two flamboyant, absurd ideas which he wrote about with almost the same fervour he was to show on behalf of the establishment of a Jewish state. His first proposal was that he, Herzl, should challenge some of the leading anti-Semites of the day to a series of duels: in this way he would prove to them that the Jews were both brave and gentlemanly. His next brainwave was for a series of immense pageants to be staged in every capital of Europe, in the course of which the Jews would undergo mass conversion to Christianity. (But *noblesse oblige*: the leaders of the movement, Herzl included, would not be converted; they would continue to bear the stigma of being Jewish, in order to prove how disinterested their motives were in leading their people to take this step.)

The Zionist idea, as events proved, was very different from these grotesque false starts. What is more, Herzl knew it at once. But his touchiness, his passionate desire to cut a figure, the shallowness of much of his thinking about society and history, the difficulty he had in co-operating with others, his acquiescence in many of the beliefs anti-Semites held about Jews, his concern with medals and decorations – none of these were lost when he became the demonically driven leader of a people. His yearning admiration for Prussian Junkers and English aristocrats did not diminish; on the contrary, as a result of his political campaigning he met more members of both classes than before, and revelled wistfully and boastfully in doing so.

Consider, for example, this extract from his diary, written during one of several visits he made to England:

A quiet park, a delicious garden, silence all around the venerable manor . . .

We ensconced ourselves in one of the drawing-rooms for tea. The ideal English home. Outside the windows the most gentle spring landscape; in the drawing-room, nevertheless, blazing logs in the fireplace . . . What charming jingoists these two are, proud of their beautiful England, which they call the first, finest, foremost Power in the world. *Mon avis!*

All the meanders of our conversation over five o'clock tea, later over dinner at the beautiful English table decorated with flowers . . . cannot be reproduced. These are the people, this is the milieu that I need for my well-being.

Or this, also from the diary, written during a visit to a country house in Prussia:

In a brief half-hour we were at Liebenberg. A beautiful manor house, to which a new wing is being added. I had no chance really to look around. Two footmen were waiting outside the gate. One of them announced me to the Count. In the hall hunting weapons and trophies. The whole, grand style. The Count came out at once. He was in hunting costume, and it seemed to me that the first thing he did was to take stock of my clothes. I had carefully considered what I should wear, and had taken my grey frock-coat and trousers, although under different circumstances the light-coloured lounge suit would have been more appropriate. The light-coloured suit would have been informal. However, I certainly did not want to give the impression that I considered myself a guest. I was coming on business, a shade less *habillé* than if it had been in the city – that is, grey rather than black.

I believe he found me suitably dressed.

One would have to be an exceptionally hard-hearted reader to find such diary entries *only* absurd. Parallels to the first passage could be found easily enough in the writings of a supposed super-sophisticate like Henry James. At the same time it is not surprising that when the author quoted above came to sketching out his plans for his Zion-to-be, whether in his diaries or in his 'futuristic' novel *Altneuland*, the results should invariably have been jejune: all electricity, brass bands, and well-dressed ladies and gentlemen conversing in German amid elegant Mediterranean townscapes. With a little unalarming, middle-class socialism thrown in. Though he had the largeness of spirit to recognise the strengths of East European Jewry, of whom he had been quite ignorant before, he never wholly reconciled himself to the fact that it was these despised, demi-proletarian *Ostjuden* who really rallied to him, not the classier Jews of the West.

*

Thus the unconsciously clownish aspects of his character, which pursued him throughout his own pursuit of grandeur, like some mocking shadow or anti-self, ultimately come to have an unexpected effect: they make anyone who goes

51

through the second half of the tale told by his biographer, or follows Herzl's own account of it in his diaries, marvel all the more at his energy and obduracy and capacity for self-sacrifice. There was no end to his courage in the face of repeated heartbreaks and rebuffs; to the boldness of the political feats of sleight-of-hand he attempted to carry off; to his readiness to sacrifice his personal wealth for the cause he had invented, or believed he had invented, single-handed; to the tirelessness with which he would follow up any idea, no matter how bizarre, or travel to any destination, no matter how distant, which might be of help to him in his struggle. Nor did he flinch from the knowledge that the pace he was going at was bound to kill him; more remarkably still, given his character, he went in for no heroics on that particular subject.

Essentially his campaigns were fought on two fronts simultaneously. On the one hand he had to try, through some spectacular success in his dealings with the great powers of the day, to convince the Jews of Europe that he had indeed found a solution to their problems, and that it would be worth their while to support him. On the other hand, in his meetings with kings, sultans, popes, prime ministers, foreign ministers and assorted notabilities in a host of countries, he had to pretend that the support he was seeking from the Jews was already his, and that as a result he had at his command millions of followers and (no less important) millions of francs or marks or pounds sterling. On both fronts his successes were few and far between. The Zionists he managed to gather around him were neither numerous nor wealthy; they hardly made up for these lacks by being given to interminable caucusing and bitter personal rivalries. He was cold-shouldered by the wealthy Jewish philanthropists, like the Rothschilds and the Hirschs, without whom his prospects of raising large sums of money were nil. The rabbis from one side, and the Jewish socialists from the other, fought him tooth and nail. Having set up his organisation in these unpropitious circumstances, he began a series of endless negotiations with the Sultan of Turkey, who then ruled Palestine; in effect, this meant throwing bribes wholesale down the bottomless pit of the Sultan's court (for which the financial managers of the Zionist movement did not fail to denounce him). He discussed with Joseph Chamberlain, the British Colonial Secretary, the possibility of the Jews establishing a new 'Zion' in Uganda, Cyprus, or Sinai (for which the 'Palestine-only' faction among the Zionists did not cease to revile him). To the outrage of the Russian Jews he met the anti-Semitic Tsarist minister, Plehve, and tried to canvas his support. All his schemes and travels, meetings and negotiations, came to nought. At the end of nine years he had nothing to show for his efforts but a noisy and penniless Zionist organisation, with almost as many factions as it had branches and committees. On his death-bed, in delirium, he pointed at a particular spot on the bed-clothes and instructed his secretary, '*This* piece of land – the National Fund must buy it.'

Let a single example of his hectic, fruitless endeavours stand for all the rest. (It makes up one of the saddest and most amusing chapters in Amos Elon's biography.) The Kaiser, who had Middle Eastern ambitions, announced that he was going on a pilgrimage to Palestine. Herzl, who had been working for years to interest the Kaiser in his plans, hoped in some ill-defined fashion that as a result of this journey the Sultan would grant the Kaiser a protectorate over Palestine; and that he in turn would obligingly grant the Zionists a charter enabling them to settle there and begin building the Jewish state. Through various intermediaries, some well-intentioned, some malicious, he was given to understand that it would be a good thing if he were to petition the Kaiser to that effect in Jerusalem itself. Off he rushed, in a state of euphoric expectation, to Constantinople; there he was granted an interview with the Kaiser, whose polite nothings-very-much Herzl interpreted in the most favourable possible light. Then he took the next boat to Jaffa, in order to await the Kaiser's arrival in Palestine. *En route* he had a bad fall on the ship's gangway and injured his leg. Then he caught a fever. The heat in Palestine, which he was visiting for the first time, overwhelmed him. Turkish secret policemen followed him and his colleagues everywhere. The tiny Jewish colonies he visited were poverty-stricken and unwelcoming. (*They* did not believe in his political fantasies, and were ready to continue living indefinitely on Baron Rothschild's charity.) His foot swollen, his temperature mounting steadily, subject to attacks of vomiting, irritated beyond endurance by the dust and heat, he awaited the Kaiser's arrival outside an agricultural college called Mikve Israel (the Hope of Israel). When the Kaiser arrived, in a huge mounted party, he exchanged a few more bland words with Herzl, and then rode on.

Everybody followed the imperial cavalcade to Jerusalem. The filth and smells of the Old City disgusted Herzl. After five days of waiting he and his friends were summoned to see the Kaiser again. Sweltering in their formal court-dress, the deputation came and said its piece. Out of the wisdom garnered from his trip the Kaiser remarked that what the country needed above all was 'water and trees'. Out of an older wisdom still he said that 'money is what you [Jews] have plenty of. More money than any of us.' (In his diary Herzl records that this was said 'jovially' by the Kaiser, with a slap of his riding-crop at his boot.) Not a word was uttered about charters or protectorates. Nor was anything said about them in the few lines devoted to the meeting in the official report on the pilgrimage. The Empress smiled pleasantly at Herzl, but told her confidantes that what she didn't like about Jerusalem was that there were 'so many filthy Jews' to be seen there. End of chapter; end of years of careful planning and much less careful hoping by Herzl. Back to the Sultan. Back to the British. Back to Lord Rothschild. Back to face a disappointed and bitterly critical Zionist Congress.

*

One of the photographs in Amos Elon's biography shows Herzl, solah topee in hand, waiting for the Kaiser outside Mikve Israel. He wears a dark suit. He stands quite alone, but gazes masterfully towards the horizon, like the commander of an army. There is nothing nearby but barren sand and an incongruous kitchen chair;

in the background is a dispiriting huddle of Arab-style huts. The forlorn pathos of the photograph is difficult to describe; or to contemplate.

Looking at that picture I was reminded strangely of the old illustrations I used to come across, during my schooldays in South Africa, of worthies of one sort or another proclaiming republics, negotiating treaties with bemused blacks, or solemnly extending the Queen's territories by means of a flag and a declaration. Why should Herzl have imagined that Palestine or the Middle East would be any different from the Africa of his day? The years of his most intense political activity coincided almost exactly with the 'Scramble for Africa', when an entire continent was carved up almost effortlessly between the European powers. No wonder, then, that he thought of a potentate like the Kaiser as some kind of *deus ex machina*, dispensing charters and protectorates to suitable applicants.

No wonder, too, that he should have been so interested in the career of the arch-Scrambler, Cecil John Rhodes – multi-millionaire, head of the British South African Charter Company, and Prime Minister of the Cape Colony – and should have tried repeatedly to get in touch with him. But while Englishmen like Rhodes, as well as Belgians, Frenchmen, Germans and the rest had armies and navies to deploy, Herzl had only his own preposterous dignity to depend on. (So dignified was he, indeed, that when he was in Palestine he had had eyes only for the Kaiser; none for the Arabs who actually occupied the land.) Which makes it all the more remarkable that today the state for the sake of which he stood out there in the sun, actually exists, however precariously, whereas all those empires have melted away.

The Kaiser's jovialities notwithstanding, Herzl did not even have any money at his disposal. However unfair it may be to compare men so differently placed, the contrast with Rhodes is again instructive. Rhodes, who succeeded in dragging the British government in London into one imperial adventure after another, did not begin his political career until he had amassed his fortune in the South African diamond and gold fields. He had no shame in setting out quite deliberately to make a fortune, with the express intention of using it later to further his grandiose, indeed megalomaniac, political ambitions. ('I would annex the planets if I could.') In response to an approach by one of the intermediaries Herzl sent him, Rhodes spoke candidly enough: 'If Mr Herzl wants a tip from me, tell him to put money in his purse.' His advice could not have been better – or more beside the point. Herzl, the Jewish writer, intellectual and dandy, could never have gone about things as Rhodes had done. Prior to Herzl's political awakening he had despised money-making: among other reasons because it was so 'Jewish'. He was far too aristocratic and literary in his tastes. The result? Once in politics, he was constantly having to go cap-in-hand to those unsympathetic Jewish magnates who had shown themselves less refined in their sensibilities than he; and he was never able to make the offer of hard cash to the Sultan which he believed (perhaps wrongly) might have made a crucial difference to their negotiations.

The involutions and ironies of Herzl's fate as a man, a writer, and a political leader, do not end there. It was precisely the exacerbation of that delicate and wounded sensibility of his, which he had cherished as evidence of having been marked out for literary fame, that eventually drove him into politics, where he revealed how much steel there was in his character. And, paradoxically enough, it was his brutally 'unaesthetic' and unrewarding political life which provided him with the materials and the passion to write the one book which can today sustain the reader's interest, when all the rest of the literary work he had set so much store by, plays, novels and essays alike, has turned to dross and tedium. I refer not to *The Jewish State*, which is merely an outdated pamphlet, a call to action, but to the series of private diaries he began when his obsession took hold of him. To the first of them he prefixed the bold title, *Book One: Of the Jewish Cause: Begun in Paris: Around Pentecost 1895*. It is extraordinary how, throughout the years that followed, with all their disappointments and failures, he managed to maintain something of the tone of manic excitement we find in its opening paragraph:

> For some time I have been occupied with a work of infinite grandeur. At the moment I do not know if I will carry it through. It looks like a mighty dream. But for days and weeks it has possessed me beyond the limits of my consciousness; it accompanies me wherever I go, hovers behind my ordinary talk, looks over my shoulder at my comically trivial journalistic work, disturbs me and intoxicates me.

At every moment his impossible schedule allowed him, he scribbled down impressions, speculations, drafts of speeches and articles, sardonic asides ('Then we went to lunch [in the Sultan's palace] and ate Turkish dishes which had been warm once'), and whatever else came into his head. The effect is to compel us, as readers of the diaries, to witness his 'work of infinite grandeur', his 'mighty dream', being translated back, so to speak, into daylight, on to the plane of 'ordinary talk' and 'trivial work'. Only on that plane could it ever have become anything other than a dream, as Herzl knew from the very day his obsession took hold of him. Look with what a longingly ambiguous, backward glance he bids farewell, in the opening entry of his diary, to his career as a creator of literary fictions – a career which this, by far the grandest of his creations, was soon to abort forever:

> It is too early to surmise what will come of it. But my experience tells me that even as a dream it is something remarkable, and that I ought to write it down – if not as a reminder to mankind, then at least for my own delight or reflection in later years. And perhaps as something between these two possibilities – that is, literature. If my conception is not translated into reality, at least out of it may come a novel. Title: The Promised Land!

*

In the Epilogue to his *Herzl*, Amos Elon reminds us that below Herzl's tomb in Jerusalem, on the hill which now carries his name, stretches one of the largest military cemeteries in Israel. There lie the bodies of thousands of young men who died in successive wars fought by the state he did so much to call into being. On the western slope of that hill is the Yad Vashem, the memorial to the six million slaughtered Jews of Europe, whom the state came into existence too late to save.

SEVEN

THE BRONTËS, AGAIN

———◆———

Different though they are from one another, it is hardly insulting to the Brontës' novels to describe them collectively as restitutive or consolatory fantasies. That is, they are the means through which each of the sisters, conscious of gifts thwarted or disregarded and of opportunities denied, was able imaginatively to live a life richer, more active, and more rewarding than any she had been permitted to experience in her own being. In endowing their heroines with passions and capacities which the authors wished at the same time to know for themselves and to make known to others, they had to endow them also with a social and physical arena in which these qualities could be displayed; an arena filled with fierce lovers and enemies, with idle or concerned spectators, with argument, drama and incertitude.

But that is not the only sense in which one can speak of their fictions providing the authors with opportunities and excitements of a kind they could not hope to experience in any other fashion, given their situation as penurious, unmarried young women living in an extreme degree of social and intellectual isolation. Weaving fantasies, writing poems and tales for one another's entertainment, had been something they had done since childhood. Attempting to transform this familial game into the similar and yet radically different activity of writing novels and of seeking to become known as novelists, or of writing poems with the intention of trying to become known as poets, was itself the expression of a wish or hunger, part of the search for a mode of escape from the circumstances in which they appeared to be imprisoned; one that would be achieved, if at all, through making public that which they knew as potentiality within themselves.

Not that the attempt would come easily to them. How could it? Among the many dreads they had – one that was to seem all too thoroughly justified by the wretched reception of the book of poems they published jointly as Currer, Ellis, and Acton Bell, and the contemptuous critical response given to *Wuthering Heights* and *The Tenant of Wildfell Hall* – was that their wish to become known as artists might itself prove to be no more than yet another fantasy, another unreality. If that turned out to be the case, then this particular dream would have revealed itself to be that which dreams always threaten to become – ultimately a form of imprisonment rather than of escape – and they would have succeeded only in locking themselves more firmly than ever into the psychological and material privations from which they had been seeking to emerge.

*

Anybody may blame me who likes, when I add further, that, now and then, when I took a walk by myself in the grounds; when I went down to the gates and looked through them along the road; or when, while Adèle played with her nurse, and Mrs Fairfax made jellies in the storeroom, I climbed the three staircases, raised the trapdoor of the attic, and having reached the leads, looked out afar over sequestered field and hill, and along dim skyline – that then I longed for a power of vision which might overpass that limit; which might reach the busy world, towns, regions full of life I had heard of but never seen; that then I desired more of practical experience than I possessed; more of intercourse with my kind, of acquaintance with variety of character, than was here within my reach. I valued what was good in Mrs Fairfax, and what was good in Adèle; but I believed in the existence of other and more vivid kinds of goodness, and what I believed in I wished to behold.

Who blames me? Many, no doubt; and I shall be called discontented. I could not help it; the restlessness was in my nature; it agitated me to pain sometimes. Then my sole relief was to walk along the corridor of the third story, backwards and forwards, safe in the silence and solitude of the spot, and allow my mind's eye to dwell on whatever bright visions rose before it – and, certainly, they were many and glowing; to let my heart be heaved by exultant movement, which, while it swelled in trouble, expanded it with life; and, best of all, to open my inward ear to a tale that was never ended – a tale my imagination created and narrated continuously; quickened with all the incident, life, fire, feeling, that I desired and had not in my actual existence.

This passage from *Jane Eyre* might be said to express in Charlotte Brontë's own terms and with her own especial vehemence precisely the view of her and her sisters' fictions outlined above. Notice particularly the way in which she presents the dialectic between deprivation and creation, frustration and the exercise of the imagination, isolation and appetite. (It was only when she was *safe* in what she describes with a curious alliterative insistence as 'the silence and solitude of the spot' that her heart 'heaved . . . swelled . . . expanded' and she was able to launch herself on the creation of that 'tale that was never ended'.) The passage describes exactly what the novel is doing for the author and what she herself is doing within the novel; and all this without losing its dramatic appropriateness or convincingness as part of the stream of thought of the fiercely articulate starveling (emotionally speaking) who is in fact not the author of the book but its heroine. It should also be noted that the activity of dreaming and narrating is itself seen here by the author, if not by Jane herself, as a vital element of Jane's 'actual existence'; the 'vision' and the 'passion' she longs for may appear to her to be out of her reach, but we have been put in a position to know better. In speaking of them as she has just done, she has revealed herself to be their seat or carrier in the novel; they turn out to be its very substance, that which it contains, expresses, and has come into being to manifest.

Much the same could be said of the specifically 'feminist' reflections which Charlotte Brontë puts in the mouth of her heroine in the very next paragraph. 'Women are supposed to be very calm generally,' she tells us, whereas in fact they 'feel just as men feel; they need exercise for their faculties, and a field for their efforts as much as their brothers do.' The novel itself provides more than just the context of these remarks; simply by being what it is, it proves in the most incontrovertible fashion the truth of the case they are making.

The complexities of telling 'endless' or 'continuous' tales of this kind, as Jane calls them, do not end there, however. Certainly, the tale or novel is a form of restitution made by its creator, to its creator, for what she feels she has missed in her life. But all that is left unaltered and unmitigated in that life will in due course (or rather, simultaneously) demand restitution from the novel – i.e. *within* the novel – for the fact that the restitution has been made in fantasy only. The heroine who does what the author wishes to do, or experiences what the author wishes her to experience, will not only have the benefit throughout of the author's sympathy, but will feel the brunt of her chagrin and envy as well. If the book is 'quickened' by the desires enacted in it, we can be sure that it will be quickened also by the reproaches the author will feel herself obliged to utter, in one form or another, against herself and her characters, for having indulged in such desires, or provided the occasion for them, or indeed simply for having been in a position, unlike the author, where such indulgence is possible. The act of reproach must therefore also be seen, in its turn, in its many turns, as being expressive of desire at a different level. And the relationship between all these contradictory and self-confounding desires, at all these levels, is of course never for a moment static or stable; they are constantly changing not just their places with one another, but their very nature.

*

Though Emily Brontë's one work of fiction is in many respects unlike the various novels written by Charlotte, the relevance to *Wuthering Heights* of much of what has been said (and quoted) above is, I hope, apparent. Emily was the quietest and most restrained, the most homeloving of all the sisters, the one least able to cope with outside faces and outside places. Her novel depicts, with an unconcealed element of defiance and exultation, an unrestrained passion of love between a man and woman who have no real regard for anyone but themselves or for anything but their own feelings. None the less, in the light of what has just been said, we can hardly be surprised at the fact that the lovers are not only admired but are severely punished too, through sufferings that are presented in the novel as 'self-inflicted', as the necessary consequence of all they do to themselves and others in their headlong pursuit of their passion.

However, almost as important to the novel, it seems to me, if we are thinking of it as a restitutive fantasy, is the author's translation in it of the life she had known in the Haworth vicarage into something different and more interesting; something more 'literary', anyway. I use the last adjective without any derogatory intention: quite the contrary. Anyone brought up in deeply provincial circumstances will be familiar with a trick that is sometimes used by people with a particular kind of temperament to render their surroundings more hospitable, imaginatively speaking, to their own needs. The trick is simply *not* to take for granted the scenes they have known best and longest, but to try to think of them as the strange, demi-mythical *terra incognita* which they might appear to be to someone who comes from elsewhere, preferably from the metropolis, and who is filled with wonder to see how different things are in this part of the world. (The metropolis might be defined here as that region where everything is at one with the descriptions that have been offered of it.)*

For a novelist to use this trick in order to see her own locale, and to make the reader see it, as some kind of cultural and topographical anomaly, as a place needing explanation or awaiting the confirmation of an outsider's gaze, is to do more than defy the metropolis while at the same time truckling to it. It is also a means whereby the novelist can assert the validity of her own deepest experience, even of her own sense of herself, while implicitly confessing her anxieties about both. Hence the importance of the presence in *Wuthering Heights* of the effete, goggling, urban Lockwood, who has to be instructed in the climate of the moors and the habits and passions of the moor-dwellers, even as he in effect instructs them in the social assumptions and expectations of the metropolis.

Strange though it may seem to say so, a rather similar consideration arises in this novel, as it does in many others, with the depiction of certain kinds of solitary suffering. The point is that if you can manage to make such suffering a part of a story you are telling, if you can make something resembling a work of art out of it, then, like those hitherto undescribed landscapes, it will have become different from what it was before, and more interesting; like those landscapes, it might even be transformed into that for which people more fortunately placed than yourself can come to envy you. They will be forced to think of you as someone who has had experiences denied to them and who possesses a hard-won knowledge of which they have been deprived. And of course if the story you produce is genuinely a work of art, it will manage not only to express suffering of this kind but also your misgivings about the uses to which you are now putting it,

---

* The essay on Olive Schreiner which appears below is obviously relevant here: indeed, the 'case' of Olive Schreiner has more than just this in common with Emily Brontë's.

and whatever doubts you have, consciously or unconsciously, about the consolations you are trying to wring out of it.

None of what has just been said is peripheral to that part of the novel which is concerned with the love between Heathcliff and Catherine, the untamed and untameable couple who cannot live without each other and who eventually, in their different fashions, out of their differing solitudes and frustrations, can be said to be responsible for each other's deaths. (It is a special sort of slow-motion killing that Catherine ultimately inflicts on Heathcliff.) As far as Heathcliff is concerned, his paternity in the novel may be a mystery, but his literary descent, from the hero-villains of the Gothic fictions of the previous century, has often been remarked on – and even, occasionally, derided. The same is true of his connection with the life and the poems of the wicked Lord Byron, who, along with such figures as the Duke of Wellington and Napoleon, had been an important participant in the elaborate story-games with which the Brontë children had busied themselves over many years.

Catherine, on the other hand, has generally been seen in quite a different way, as a character virtually without precedent, and (at least until the publication of Q.D. Leavis's essay in *Lectures in America*) as one that should be taken 'straight'; indeed, regarded with a kind of awe. For her part, Mrs Leavis sees the novel as a severely 'moral' tome, in which Catherine's famous outbursts of passion are viewed with strict disfavour by the author, who presents the younger Cathy as a sane, admirable counterpoint and antitype to her wracked mother. The novel is 'moral in intention' Mrs Leavis argues, because 'the author's preferences are shown . . . [and] the reader is obliged to draw moral conclusions'. Chief among these improving conclusions is that the younger Cathy 'develops the maturity and therefore achieves the happiness that her mother failed in'.

I have already amply indicated that in my view the moral life of the novel resides not in any 'conclusions' or precepts that may be drawn from it, not even those which the author herself may have intermittently wished us to draw, but precisely in the passionate ambivalences out of which it emerges and which it compels us, as readers, to live through. Catherine is seen by the author to be, among other things, a spoiled child and a wilful wrecker of the lives of the people around her; she is also loved and admired and envied by the author for daring to be all that she disapproves of. Only thus could Catherine become wholly the person she has it within herself to become – which is to say, only thus could she engage wholly the imaginative powers of her creator – and remain what she is to the very end, when she and Heathcliff lie together in calmly Wordsworthian (but also spooky and Gothic) fashion under the grass of the windblown moors. Had the novelist not been so deeply divided, there would have been little or nothing within her that could be united only in the form of a work of the imagination, and so there would have been no novel; or if there were one it would have been as weak and wishful and as lacking in power as the happy ending (brought about by the 'maturity' and 'wisdom' of the young Cathy) actually turns out to be.

One last point. Heathcliff has been described so often as a Byronic character that it has been overlooked that there is another, and much more interesting and successful, Byronic figure in the book: namely, Catherine herself. (When she exclaims, in what is perhaps the most famous sentence in the book, 'I *am* Heathcliff', she is not only expressing an extremity of romantic passion; I cannot help feeling that she is also unwittingly proffering us a piece of cultural analysis.) It is true that she is not dark or of mysterious provenance or given to unfathomable disappearances and strange oaths. All else aside, she is a woman, and the boundaries within which she can move are correspondingly narrower. But she is Byronic in the sense that her power and fascination over others lies at every stage in the primacy which she gives – or appears to give – to her own emotions, without regard for moral constraints; she is Byronic too in her duplicity.

To have been able to create a Byronic woman was in itself a remarkable achievement; to go on to submit her to a close examination, as the novelist could not begin to do with a man like Heathcliff, seems to me more remarkable still. It is as if she asks: from where do these people get their energy? What do they do to themselves and to other people in giving vent to these energies? And the surprising answer she comes up with is that the source of their energy is not in their emotions, as they would wish to have us believe, but in their will to dominate others. Or perhaps one should say: that is their primary emotion. They destroy the people around them rather than let them go free; if all else fails, they destroy themselves, in a perversity of self-assertion. ('My soul will be on that hilltop before you lay hands on me again.') It follows that at some level they know themselves to be fakes, for they know that the passions by which they claim to be ruled, and by which they rule others, are instrumental, a means to an end. Nelly Dean says as much in speaking of Catherine, when she describes her as one who is adept in 'turning [her] fits of passion to account'.

But then it is also Nelly Dean, again speaking of Catherine, who tells us, 'Well, we *must* be for ourselves in the end.' Those are words which the heroine of the novel might have been glad to use about herself; ultimately we come to recognise how fully they fit the novelist, too.

PART THREE

RUSSIAN

EIGHT

TOLSTOY YOUNG AND OLD

◆

As a very young man Tolstoy volunteered to take part, with his older brother, in a small war against rebellious tribesmen in the Caucasus. Here is an extract from a letter he wrote to his brother, while waiting for a transfer from the town of Tiflis.

I told you I need 100 roubles to get away; now I see I shan't manage without 140. Help me as much as you can. Perhaps you think I'm quite well now. Unfortunately I'm very unwell. La maladie venérienne est détruite, mais ce sont les suites du Mercure qui me font souffre l'impossible. Just imagine, my mouth and tongue are completely covered in sores, which prevents me eating and sleeping. Without any exaggeration, this is the second week I've eaten nothing, and I haven't slept a single hour. All these horse doctors and scoundrels! It's a good thing there are waters here, and God willing, I'll get better somehow.

I was going to write you about a very interesting matter, but I'm so tired I'll go off to bed. I'll write by the next post, or, if I have time, I'll add something more. It's not worth giving the white horse away for 13 roubles. Goodbye. Don't forget to forward all letters and send me as much money as you can.

And here is Tolstoy, the world-famous novelist and sage, the pacifist, teetotaller, vegetarian, anarchist, and believer in chastity, instructing his son, Misha, aged sixteen, to put off for at least seven years his projected marriage to a peasant girl with whom he had fallen in love:

In those seven years you should stop learning to play the accordion and to dance, and should inure yourself to every form of abstinence and hard work, and in addition, should not only not sink lower in mental and moral development, but should raise and consolidate yourself so as to raise your wife in this respect too; [and] you and she should live for these seven years chastely, without ceasing to work on yourselves . . .

Pleasure comes as a reward only to the man who doesn't make it the goal of his life. When a man makes it his goal in life, the opposite always happens, he destroys life: you get debauchery, illness, onanism, or that stupefying state of being in love which you have succumbed to and its inevitable consequence; the crippling of body and soul and the incapacity of any type of enjoyment. Vodka, tobacco, and other means of stupefaction such as the accordion invariably accompany this frame of mind because, by befogging the reason, they hide from a man the falseness of his goal.

The contrast between the letters appears plain enough, at first sight. On the one hand there is the dissipated, bankrupt cadet, full of mercury and self-pity; on the other, the moralist and preacher strenuously urging on someone else a way of life totally unlike any he had been capable of following at that age. The gap between the young man and the old seems immense, even unbridgeable. However, a little reflection suggests that the continuities and resemblances between them are hardly less striking than the differences. Both men are deeply self-absorbed: the advice-giving father quite as much as the gonorrheal, money-cadging brother, for only someone who had altogether forgotten what it was like to be young could ever have adopted such a tone in writing to a sixteen-year-old. Each man appears to be wholly incapable of imagining himself to be other than he is at the very moment of writing; in neither letter is there a trace of irony, self-distance, or humour – ludicrous though both letters undoubtedly are. In both cases the writer is convinced that *he* is in the right in whatever he feels and wants, and that all others around him are in the wrong, whether they be the horse doctors and scoundrels plaguing the subaltern, or the accordionists and onanists whom the aged prophet sees everywhere around him.

In short, both letters appear to have been written by some kind of moral simpleton. If the gulf between the subaltern and the elderly sage seems (initially at least) to yawn so widely, what then is one to make of the disjuncture between the letter-writer and the man whom we know to have been one of the greatest imaginative writers who has ever lived? No novelist has created a greater range of characters of different classes and dispositions than Tolstoy; in his letters one looks in vain for any sense of the living presence of either the people he writes about or the people to whom the letters are addressed. No one has written better than Tolstoy about the exhilaration of physical activity – riding a sleigh, kissing a girl through a window, running across a field in the midst of an artillery bombardment; nothing of the kind appears in the letters. (In the same letter to Misha Tolstoy in which he comes down so heavily on accordion playing, he solemnly classifies bicycle riding as a 'vice'.) The evocation of intense and sustained states of happiness, always considered one of the most difficult of a novelist's tasks, is something that Tolstoy achieves over and over again in his fiction; in his letters he is usually miserable and disgruntled, if not actually in despair, for one reason or another. No writer, again, is better than Tolstoy in presenting the traumatised stillness of the mind in moments of extreme danger or fatigue, the clumsiness and intensity with which it labours to follow the unhesitating reflexes and responses of the body; in the letters the omnipotence of the conscious will over both body and mind is assumed or at least asserted at all times. (The will itself, however, is in turn seen as coming under the iron constraint of various unalterable, *a priori*, ethical precepts.) The novels are full of lyrical evocations of nature at different seasons; the letters by and large are bare of them.

When we turn from the direct evidence of the letters to that of the biographies the same paradoxes emerge. This is as true of a work written by a contemporary and follower of Tolstoy, like Aylmer Maude, as it is of one by a modern 'professional' like Henri Troyat. It is true also of the memoirs of those who visited the Tolstoy home at Yasnaya Polana (and almost everyone who visited it seems to have felt obliged to put down his or her impressions), or of those, like Tolstoy's favourite daughter, Tatyana, who were born into the household. From Henri Troyat, for example, we learn that among the books on subjects close to his heart which Tolstoy planned to write as a young man were 'Foundations of Music and Rules for its Study', 'On Gymnastics' and 'On Cards'. (The size of his gambling debts presumably showed what an expert he was on the last of these topics.) These unfulfilled projects were at odds with, and yet also at one with, the very different ambitions that constantly compelled him to fill his diaries with innumerable lists of 'Rules of Life'. Later, when he had had his first works published, he also set about drawing up 'Rules of Writing'. Always the mania for rules! And always the incapacity to live by them for any longer than it took to write them down. 'I am living like a beast,' an early entry in his diary records. 'In the evening drew up precepts, then went to the gypsies.' (Anything less beast-like than either activity it would be hard to imagine, actually; let alone both of them at once.) Sixty years later, with all his ineradicable appetite and aggression, he was intent on devoting himself and everyone around him, whether they liked it or not, to his doctrines of pacifism, poverty, chastity, simplicity, and, above all, self-abnegation . . . 'I have rarely met a man who is more endowed with all the vices than I,' reads an entry in one of his very last diaries: 'voluptuousness, self-interest, malice, vanity, and especially self-love. I thank God that I know this . . . and am still struggling against it. This is what explains the success of my writings.'

In speaking of his 'success' at that point it was his later, didactic writings that Tolstoy had in mind. By then he had abjured the works for which he is now remembered and revered; he had also in effect abjured his wife, most of his family, and (notionally at least) everything he owned. The consequences for him and for those around him make up one of the most famous episodes of literary biography: understandably so, for it is a mixture of cautionary tale, tragedy, and farce, which it is impossible to go through, in the various versions proffered of it – including Tolstoy's own – without feeling a kind of despairing fascination, along with a somewhat guilty mirth. Over the years, Yasnaya Polana, which had been the scene of so many family idylls, was transformed into a place of torment and grotesque comedy, with everyone in it feverishly recording every move in the struggles that were going on for the soul and property of the dazed but unrelenting old man. On one side were the so-called 'Tolstoyans', led by Tolstoy's editor and confidant, Chertkov, and including Tatyana in their number. In the name of all the lofty causes Tolstoy had espoused – of course – they wanted him to be theirs and theirs alone; they wanted to control everything he did and everything he published and all the money that accrued to him, or would accrue to his family, from every source. On the other side was Sophia Andreyevna, who had been married to him for almost fifty years, supported by many of her children, who wanted to enjoy her rights and privileges as the wife of the world's most famous writer. They fought over his diaries (his 'official' diary, his secret diary, his secret-secret diary), his copyrights, his will; they huddled him off to confidential meetings in the depths of the woods; the members of the opposing camps met each other in grand, tear-drenched, Russian embraces and reconciliations, which broke up after ten minutes into oaths and threats of litigation. In the end, when the dying reformer of all mankind tried to run away from the domestic situation he himself had done so much to create, it was inevitable that he should be followed to his death-bed at the wayside railway station of Astapovo by his family, by the gang of Tolstoyans, and by what Boris Pasternak, who was there with his father, was to call in his *Essay in Autobiography* 'the braying camp of the world's press'. All that was missing were television cameras.

*

Which brings one back to the subject of Tolstoy's 'simplicity'; a simplicity rightly recognised by admirers of his novels (the novels he had come to despise) as one of the greatest sources of his strength. Anyone who has been through the documents and considered the story they tell is likely to find himself asking the question about the disjuncture between the man and the novelist in very different terms from those used earlier in this essay. In fact, the emphasis will now fall on what one insistently feels to be the connection between Tolstoy's capacity to be wholly himself, even remorselessly himself, whatever that self might happen to be at different stages of his career, and the capacity of the novelist to fill the consciousness of his characters with a sense of their own autonomy and significance. (In *Tolstoy and the Novel* John Bayley introduces us to a Russian word for this quality: *samolodnovost*, meaning self-sufficiency or self-esteem.) In rather the same way that one began to recognise his startlingly unchanged lineaments in the apparently revolutionary transformations he went through on his journey from subaltern to world reformer to pathetic runaway, so one eventually comes to feel that the secret of his chameleonic power as a novelist has to be found, paradoxically enough, in his very self-absorption. For if it is not there, where else might it be found? What was it that enabled this overweeningly self-preoccupied and self-willed man to produce those subtle, beautiful and capacious novels – which, if any novels do, fully deserve D.H. Lawrence's encomium of the genre as 'the highest example of subtle *inter-relatedness* man has discovered'? (My italics.)

The first answer one is tempted to give, inevitably, is that Tolstoy appears to be a man who did not need to invent anything at all when he wrote, since he merely had to look inside himself in order to find every one of his characters there: from the shyest, purest youth (or girl) to the most profligate drunkard and whoremonger; from the undemanding, easily amused peasant to the alienated, self-aggravated intellectual; from the smoothest courtier and social climber to the most stubbornly isolated moralist; from soldier to pacifist, passionate huntsman to vegetarian, humble pilgrim to haughty aristocrat, great artist to furious despiser of art. ('*Macbeth*', he tells us in one of his late letters, 'is a farcical play written by a clever actor with a good memory who has read a lot of clever books.') In pursuing this approach one would add, of course, that inside him too were those characters, of whom there are many in his novels, who are painfully aware that they have irreducible elements of some of the others in their makeup.

The difficulty with this argument, in my view, is that it just does not go far enough; it is insufficiently radical in its conception of 'character' as we encounter it in Tolstoy's novels, or, for that matter, in the evidence we have about the man himself. A more persuasive way of putting the matter is to say that any one of the human possibilities within him was capable of assuming so imperious a sway over his consciousness, at any moment, that it would reach right down to his quasi-instinctive, quasi-physical modes of apprehending the world and the people in it. These are the habits of apprehension and response which are most individual to each of us, though by definition we can seldom if ever be wholly aware of them, for they are not so much an expression of character as that which ultimately determines the forms our characters and personalities assume. In Tolstoy's case the personality which issued from one mode of apprehension would always be inclined to regard another as (at best) unreal and lacking in weight or (at worst) incomprehensible and a source of threat. At any rate, the most remarkable feature of his novels is that that is the level at which the people he created are given to perceiving and reacting to one another, and thus of revealing themselves to our gaze. (Inadvertently, as it were.) Think, for example, how the eternally dissatisfied seekers after truth in his novels regard the smoothies and social puppets they meet; but think also of how he is able to show us, with equal dramatic urgency and conviction, from within, the view that these social creatures have of the truth-seekers.

Tolstoy's ultimate renunciation of his art, and his denunciation of his own greatest works, do therefore have a logic to them that is not derived entirely from the religious conversion he underwent in late middle age and which he chose to see as the central event of his life. He claimed that he rejected his novels because they were about worldly matters – sex, ambition, power, social success and failure – whose worthlessness he had at last come to realise. Others were also to claim on his behalf that the very intensity of the ethical earnestness which had always been present in the novels, and which had helped to make them so affecting, inevitably carried him into another type of discourse; that it was inevitable and admirable that he should seek to speak more directly to his audience and to have an immediate and unequivocal effect on its moral conduct. But more pressing still must surely have been another set of considerations. The mutually disruptive presence within him of irreconcilable forces and impulses and modes of apprehension could not be 'disposed of', as people like to say, or 'dealt with' or 'done away with' or 'shed' in his fiction. On the contrary. The truth of the matter was that they were given a new and different life, even an eternal life if you like, by being transformed into the mutually supportive tensions and contradictions without which the novels would have had no shape, no drama, no vigour; indeed no 'proportion' and no 'harmony', to use two sweeter terms which Tolstoy himself repeatedly used, even in his late, reformed days, to describe what he looked for in literary art.

Well, if *that* was all they were good for, then let them be destroyed! If no unequivocal rules emerged from them – or something much worse, only evidence for the 'rule' that each of us is ultimately compelled to live in a world given to us and made by us through habits of apprehension that are beyond our conscious control or even our conscious knowledge – then we would be better off without them. At the very least, who can blame him for feeling that he himself would be better off without those artistic glorifications of the implacably opposing selves which, over a lifetime, had constituted his self?

And if we are to be entirely honest with ourselves, should we not admit to a sneaking sympathy with his disappointment and even disgust at imaginative literature for its power to move us and hold us and convince us of the truth of its representations; and then to leave us just as we were before – except for knowing that we have been through the experience it provided of being so held and moved and convinced? I can remember vividly the naïve disappointment I felt at the end of *War and Peace* – which had gripped me so intensely that, like a child, I had positively begrudged the time spent away from it – when I realised that the book had taken up my life for weeks on end without actually making it any easier for me to manage the rest of my life, now that I was to be left on my own once more.

'One cannot', Tolstoy wrote desperately, after the death of Dostoevsky, 'set on a pedestal for the edification of posterity a man who was all struggle.' He knew it; he was right in spite of himself. Men who are 'all struggle' provide posterity not with 'edification'; only, sometimes, with literature.

NINE

ISAAC BABEL: A JEWISH COSSACK

Reading Tolstoy I always have the feeling that the world is writing through him, that the existence of a great number of the most varied people – and not only people, but animals, plants, clouds, mountains, and constellations – has been poured out on paper through him. How can I put this more clearly? You know what a conductor is in physics. Well, as in electricity there are writers who are almost ideal conductors. Tolstoy was an ideal conductor. It's wrong to think that a talent for writing is a matter of being able to think up abstruse, startling epithets and metaphors. That used to be my trouble, and I still have to squash those metaphors in what I write, just as some not very clean people squash the vermin they find in themselves.

Poor Isaac Babel! What naïveté! He had no idea that decades after his death a multinational cohort of literary academics – some Slavs, many Frenchmen, a hundred thousand Americans, a few determined Britons toiling along behind, with the grim faces and unsteady gait of fun-runners caught in a marathon – would solemnly abolish the idea of the 'text' as a representation of a reality outside itself, or even as an attempt to achieve such a representation. He had no inkling that these authorities would also do away with the idea of the writer himself as anything other than a kind of depersonalised 'space' or 'absence' within which various linguistic 'systems' somehow come together to produce those mysteriously self-referential poems and fictions which only fully tenured members of the academic cohort are empowered to investigate. All Babel's effort to define the gifts that, for him, marked out Tolstoy's work from that of other writers; all the admiration he has for Tolstoy's capacity to let the 'world' write through him; all the self-critical zeal he shows in trying to improve what he imagined to be his own style, his own mode of transmitting to the reader the contours and pressures of what he felt to be forever beyond him . . . all of it so painfully uninstructed, so pitifully misdirected. Imagine: if only Stalin (who also fancied himself as an authority on linguistics) had known that Isaac Babel, the writer, was just one more hole in a network of intertextuality, that his sense of his ineluctably separate selfhood as an author, as an 'I', was a mere linguistic convention – if only Stalin had known all this, he might never have gone to the trouble of first silencing him and then of doing him to death. He might have saved the cost of a bullet!

All right, enough sarcasm. Even the most purblind, unreconstructed deconstructionist should be able to see that the passage by Babel quoted above is anything but naïve in what it explicitly asserts and in what it implies. (Or to put it another way: in what it both says and does.) The image of the writer as a conductor of a force like electricity, through which the essence or being of humans and non-humans alike is transmitted to the page, is anything but a blank or passive one: it speaks of power, and of the danger which springs from it. As for what Babel says about the faults of his style – well, it is hard to deny that some, perhaps even much, of his work is marred by the search for abstruse, startling metaphors, by his striving for unpredictable collocations of words and images. However, he is almost certainly wrong in imagining that he could ever have written in any other manner. Notice how startling and violent are the metaphors he uses, in this apparent appeal for plainness: first, that of the writer as a conduit for electricity, and second, that of metaphors and similes as 'vermin' which it is the duty of the writer, like an infested person, to squash.

Tolstoy came of an ancient, aristocratic Russian family; he was a landowner and a patriot; it was natural to him that he should have served in a Cossack regiment on the first occasion he went to war. Babel was a bespectacled Jewish intellectual from Odessa, born of a humble, ambitious, pacific father who, like many another Odessa Jew, nurtured the pathetic dream of seeing his son win fame and fortune by performing wonders on the violin. Like all other Russian Jews, the Babel family was burdened with distant and recent memories of pogroms, and of the part played in them by Cossack horsemen. Indeed, one of Babel's finest (and longest) stories was to show his father down on his knees, beseeching help from the indifferent commander of a Cossack squadron, with the smoke and blood of a pogrom all around them, and the mutilated body of his Grandfather Shoyl lying in the yard of the family house. How much of the story is 'fact' it is impossible to say: we know, certainly, that Babel dates the pogrom exactly (1905), soon after his tenth birthday, when such pogroms did take place in Nikolayev, his earliest place of residence, and other Russian cities; we know also that he uses his family's real name in the story. But the historical truth or otherwise of the events described in the story, however curious we may be about it, does not affect the point at issue here: which is the image that Babel the child, the man, and the writer, had of Jews and Cossacks and the relation between them. Nothing less than a revolution and a civil war had to take place for a man from such a background to ride into battle (as a war correspondent, admittedly, rather than as a trooper) with a regiment of Cossacks. And only a revolutionary prose, or a prose in a state of civil war with itself, could express so improbable a conjunction of circumstances.

It is precisely that crazed incongruity, as he sees it, of his being where he was, in such company, as Jew and Cossack, intellectual and soldier, revolutionary and cynic, aesthete and butcher (or at least comrade-in-arms of butchers), that accounts, I think, for some of the hectic gaiety of the stories in *Red Cavalry*. The collection arose directly from the campaigning he did in the Ukraine in 1920, when he and his companions pursued Polish and White Russian troops across vast tracts of territory in the Ukraine, or were pursued by them, and both sides indulged in indiscriminate pillage, rape, and slaughter of the hapless civilians they found themselves among. It is not the horrors of war that Babel delights in, though delight is an emotion we are astonished to feel at work in the pages; or even the physical courage and prowess that war calls forth, though he makes plain how much he values them. It is rather his conviction that he has found a way of writing about his war which is as distinctive, even as improbable, as his role within it. Of course he was aware of his debts to other action-writers, as one might call them: most notably de Maupassant, Tolstoy of course, and Kipling, whose 'steely prose . . . as accurate as a military report or a bank cheque' he much admired. But outrage transformed into gaiety, into a kind of mad mingling of relish, incredulity, and contempt: that is his distinctive contribution to the literature of war.

Red Cavalry is an amazing work: sufficient in itself to establish the author as one of the major figures of twentieth-century Russian literature. Yet its success is bought at a high price: it is often strained, self-conscious, rigorously limited in what it will allow itself to present of the author's experience. The last will perhaps seem a bizarre charge to make against a book so full of horrors, of deliberate or casual slaughters, of cruelties and savage humiliations inflicted at random on the guilty and innocent alike. Furthermore, Babel leaves us in no doubt that he actually envies the capacity of the people around him *not to care* about the consequences to themselves or to others of what they do; and this envy becomes another source of the strength in the book, another of the contradictions that the work itself is obliged to resolve. For if the author were really able to share his characters' insouciance, he would have no occasion to write about them and no desire to do so: not even with the grim mirth that only retrospection makes available to him.

What then is missing or excluded from the stories? Two things, I would argue. The first is that the narrator of the stories, their 'I', is never able to present directly, dramatically, within any of the individual tales in the collection, the Cossack-Jew contradiction or absurdity which is at their very heart; or to change the metaphor, is the very ground they stand on. The stories in *Red Cavalry* are not a series of disjunct tales: they are woven in and out of each other in a carefully composed manner, with many of the same people, towns, battles, wrecked homes and churches, even some of the same horses, appearing repeatedly in them. We are compelled, therefore, to see the narrator who appears in almost all of them as one person, a single character, as he moves from episode to episode. But something curious emerges in the course of this movement. It turns out that this 'I', this Jewish Cossack, is a Jew only when he is among other Jews: that is, when he takes off time from his other duties and preoccupations to visit the wretched inhabitants of the ghettoes on whom the devastation of the war has fallen. Sitting and talking to these 'old Jews with prophets' beards and passionate rags on their sunken chests', the narrator longs for the 'rotted Talmuds of his childhood', even for 'that pensioned-off Jewish God', as well as for the scraps of Jewish food which, on rare occasions, he finds to be still available among his hosts. But when he returns to the Cossacks (the Cossacks!) and goes among them, they somehow never notice that he is a Jew; they never refer to him as one; if they criticise him, or try to humiliate him, or isolate him, it is always because he is an intellectual, according to his account of it, and because they therefore feel him to be both a softie and a man with no mercy for or understanding of people like themselves.*

Now whether or not it was for political reasons, as critics have assumed, that Babel omitted to tell us how his Cossacks took to having a Jew in their midst, the consequences of the omission in terms of the stories he tells remain the same. Obviously no one is going to sit in moral judgement on the decisions Babel may have taken on what it was politically possible for him to write, or to try to publish, in the nightmarish darkness of the post-revolutionary Russia of more than sixty years ago. That is not the point. My comment refers solely to the effect on the reader of *Red Cavalry* of having the flow of his sympathies, his sense of plausibility, his attempt to recreate the fullness of the narrator's experience, blurred and switched on and off in this way. We are left willy-nilly with an awareness of a compelled and cautious reticence in a matter which is central to the subject of the stories. And that, in turn, makes us all the more likely to suspect that there is an element of bravado, a willed display of toughness, even a wish on the part of the author to make amends to himself for his silence on this central issue, in some of what the stories do go on to say.

Similar considerations apply to the second of the two elements one feels to be missing from the stories. By the very mode he has adopted, their narrator is permitted to express only a strikingly limited range of negative emotions in his confrontations with the horrors around him. Among those which are admissible from time to time are melancholy, loneliness, weariness, self-pity, squeamishness (seen only as a reason for self-reproach). Never, or at any rate very seldom, fear, disgust, horror, pity, despair. (Though words like these are in fact to be found in the published fragments of the diary that Babel kept during the Ukrainian

---

* In *You Must Know Everything* there is a draft of a story about the shooting by the Cossacks of a handful of Polish prisoners-of-war. In this draft one of the prisoners recognises the narrator as a fellow Jew, and, while the other captors look on contemptuously, turns to him for help. ('You have that nice Jewish look, sir.') The episode of the shooting of the prisoners reappears in *Red Cavalry*, but not the exchange between the Jewish prisoner and the narrator.

campaign.) It is not that one misses the words themselves on the page; if anything, the reverse is true; one admires Babel because he so steadfastly denies us, and himself, the consolation of knowing that in the midst of all this barbarism there is at least one person, the narrator, our friend, who has his heart in the right place. Yet no one, not even Babel, can get around the fact that in all imaginative literature the sensibility of the protagonist turns out to be the primary field of action; and in some of his stories, the emotion chiefly conveyed from that particular battlefield is not so much the exhilaration of the narrator as his fear of what he might feel if he allowed himself the luxury of feeling anything at all.

Thus, for all the intensity that goes into the descriptions of violent deaths in *Red Cavalry*, there is nothing in it as affecting as, for example, that moment during the noise and confusion of the battle of Borodino in *War and Peace*, when Pierre sees the death of a boy-officer who had been slightly known to him, and 'aimlessly' says to himself, 'Oh, now they will stop it, now they'll be horrified at what they've done.' He is wrong of course; so far from stopping, they have only just begun; and that too is part of the poignance of the ensign's fate and of Pierre's instinctive and useless response to it. Such a response is outside Babel's range; it would threaten the hold which he has on his prose, and which the prose has on the reader.

What creeps in instead is an aestheticising of his own shock; we can see him, as it were, making literature out of it. To say this is not to question the eerie beauty which Babel sometimes discerns in the midst of carnage, and the power with which he is capable of describing it. ('At that moment there came a tremendous and reverberating crash . . . Fires obediently rose on the horizon, and the heavy birds of the shelling flew out of the flames.' Or something as offhand and as unexpected as this: 'The tranquil dust of the bombardment rose above the earth.') Nor can one do anything but admire the elation with which he conveys moments of activity and of extreme danger, and the dilated, Russian eye he has, in the midst of turmoil, for the improbable, clinching detail. ('Bullets struck the earth and fumbled in it, quivering with impatience . . . The regimental commander, who was snoring in the sunshine, cried out in his sleep and woke up. He got into the saddle and rode off towards the vanguard squadron. His face was crumpled, lined with red streaks from his uncomfortable snooze, and his pockets were full of plums. "Damned son of a bitch!" he cried angrily, and spat a plumstone out of his mouth. "What a hell of a mess!" ' Or this description of the narrator desperately fending off an enemy soldier: 'With the palm of my hand I thrust back the face of the Kirghiz, that felt as hot as a stone in the sun.') The problem of what I have called aestheticising arises, rather, when the incongruities which are ultimately Babel's subject become a kind of *appliqué* on the surface of his prose. 'The sun oppressed by the brilliance of its own rays'; 'winding about me the straps of his smoke-hidden eyes'; 'their nailed German boots rang out with peace and hope'; 'blue roads ran past me like streams of milk spurting from many breasts' – that kind of thing.

My own feeling is that the best work Babel ever did is to be found in the group of stories he wrote about his childhood and youth in and near the city of Odessa. Neither the clenched denial of emotion which marks the tales from the battlefront, nor the overwriting in which it seems to issue, are evident here. The Odessa stories are less bloody, on the whole, than the others, but they are hardly less painful in character; while their lyricism is freer, their humour can perhaps best be described as implacable. The narrator's discovery of first love in the midst of a pogrom, the jubilation of his family when he passes an examination, the sorrowful procession to nowhere of the inmates of a Jewish poorhouse evicted by the new revolutionary authorities – all are described in terms which are at once intolerably lacerated and intolerably funny. How do the paupers mentioned in the last sentence go past the reader? Not as a spectacle but as a series of sounds only. 'The little carts of paralytics squeaked; the whistle of asthma, a humble gurgling, issued from the breasts of retired cantors, jesters at weddings, cooks at circumcisions, and ancient shop assistants.'

In an essay written in his youth, just before the revolution, and simply entitled 'Odessa', Babel showed how conscious he was of the city not merely as a fact in his own biography but as a literary idea or symbol. In the essay he called for a new, more joyful element to enter Russian literature; indeed, for nothing less than a new literary redeemer 'who should come from the sunny steppes washed by the sea.' We know what kind of a redeemer Russia as a whole actually got, and what he was to do to Russian literature and to those Russian writers, Babel among them, whose work did not find favour in his eyes. 'All went as I wished, and all went badly,' Babel wrote in a story about the most disastrous day of his childhood. Both these things could have been said about his career as a writer and as a self-divided servant of the revolution.

TEN

MANDELSTAM'S WIDOW

Osip Mandelstam was born in St Petersburg in 1891 and died in a concentration camp in Siberia towards the end of 1938, one victim among millions of others in the campaign of mass extermination that the Stalin regime was then waging against its own people. Among readers of Russian, Mandelstam's reputation as a poet has never stood higher than it does today. Those readers who have no Russian, however, are likely to come away from translations of his verse sure of only one thing about it: that it is exceptionally elliptical and allusive in nature. Certainly the poems strike an outsider like myself as being more hermetic than those of his lifelong friend, Anna Akhmatova, for example, or of his more distant and more ambiguous acquaintance, Boris Pasternak. But it also seems to be the case that his poetry became plainer and barer in style as Mandelstam grew older and the circumstances of his life grew harsher: that is to say, as he was remorselessly compelled by his murderers-to-be to go through the stations of suspicion, disfavour, banning, denunciation, arrest, dubious release, certain exile, with Siberia and the Gulag still to come. A reader has no special difficulty in sharing his poetic premonitions about what lay ahead; or, for that matter, in sympathising with his stubborn attempts to enjoy and celebrate, while it was still possible for him to do so, the life which he knew was going to be taken from him. In many of the poems he wrote in Voronezh, his last city of exile, he chose to celebrate poetry itself – the activity which his enemies most wanted to deny him, to wrest from him, and which it was not in his nature to surrender.

> You took away all the oceans and all the room.
> You gave me my shoe-size in earth with bars around it.
> Where did it get you? Nowhere.
> You left me my lips, and they shape words, even in silence.

Long before he was finally silenced, Mandelstam had also written a number of prose pieces, one of which, a substantial memoir of his childhood and early manhood entitled *The Noise of Time*, deserves much wider recognition than it has so far had in the English-speaking world. In my view it belongs wholeheartedly to that category of works which have made so much Russian writing of the nineteenth and twentieth centuries more intimately a part of the English tradition than the literature produced in any other language during the period. *The Noise of Time* is an extraordinarily rich, compressed, witty, dandified piece of writing; at once so clever and so sensuously exact that it seems again and again, with a flick of a verb or adjective, to destroy the distinctions we take for granted between a man's intellect and his sensibility, between his mind and his organs of touch or sight or smell. In *The Noise of Time* Mandelstam establishes himself at a disdainful distance from both the reader and the period he is describing ('I repeat,' he says at one point, 'my memory is not loving but inimical, and it labours not to reproduce but to distance the past'), while at the same time convincing us that this permits him to speak to us with a candour and confidentiality which would not otherwise be available to him. In rather the same way, we find that in the amused scorn of the writing about himself, his parents, grandparents, schoolmasters, even the frozen, imperial grandeurs of the city of St Petersburg, there is a tenderness he could express in no other fashion. His wit turns out to be the guarantee of his seriousness; the terseness of his style the condition of its lyrical power.

*

In 1970 there appeared in the West the first volume of Nadezhda Mandelstam's memoir of her life with her husband, *Hope Against Hope*. A second, more garrulous, and to that degree less impressive volume, *Hope Abandoned*, was published four years later. Two surprising things became evident from these books. The first was that much of the verse Mandelstam had written during the years of silence and exile before his death had survived solely because his wife had taken it on herself to learn it off by heart. All his work had gone with her, some in the form of manuscripts, some literally inside her, in her mind, during the nomadic, hand-to-mouth years of war, hunger, official disfavour and renewed purges, that had followed his imprisonment and death. The second thing to be learned from the volumes – at any rate from *Hope Against Hope*, which concentrates on, and is concentrated by, the four last years she and her husband were permitted to have together – was that Nadezhda Mandelstam was herself a writer of great gifts. In fact, in putting pen to paper for the first time, at the age of seventy, she had produced in *Hope Against Hope* a masterpiece of a kind: a book which tells us as no other has ever done just what it felt like to live as a 'civilian', as a member of the public, as the wife of a writer, a suspect, a prisoner, and then as his widow, during the blackest years of the Stalin terror.

Early in *Hope Against Hope* the author tells us that Mandelstam used to joke with one of his friends about how he would eventually die in a garret, like all ill-starred Romantic poets. Then she adds: 'But a poet is just a human being like any other, and he is bound to end up in the most ordinary way, in the way most typical of his age and times, meeting the fate that lies in wait for everyone else.' Out of context it may seem that the mingled pride and humility of this remark has something rhetorical about it. But, as with almost every other general assertion or reflection in the book, she justifies this one by showing us exactly what she believes it to mean. In the almost unbearable closing pages of the volume she describes how, two decades after her husband's death, she tried to find out, through the confused and conflicting recollections of survivors of the camps in Siberia, the exact circumstances of his death. (The only official intimation she had been vouchsafed of what had happened to him, at some undeterminable time after his arrest, was the return to her of a food parcel she had tried to send him, with a stamp on it: 'Addressee Dead'.) What her inquiries revealed to her is that she can establish nothing with any certainty about the time or place or manner of his death: not even whether any of the men whom various survivors think of as Mandelstam was really him, or some other nameless, starving, half-crazed prisoner among all those who made the journey to Siberia at that particular period. Then, remembering her earlier remark about how the fate of the poet is bound to resemble that of the people among whom he lives, the reader finds himself asking what difference it should make to *him* whether or not he ever learns exactly how Mandelstam died. What about all the others? We know about Mandelstam's dying there – of illness or hunger or a bullet through the head, who can say? – because he was a poet: a man with a considerable reputation even then; one in whom succeeding generations would be especially interested; also, as things have turned out, because he happened to have been the husband of a remarkable woman. And if none of this had been the case, would his fate have mattered any the less? Would it have been any different? How important is it in the end (or how important was it to Mandelstam himself) that his 'crime' was the writing of a poem against Stalin? ('He forges decrees in a line like horseshoes,/One for the groin, one for the forehead, temple, eye.') What were the crimes of the others?

No one will ever understand what happened in the terrible shambles of those teeming camps, where the dead with numbered tags on their legs lay side by side with the living. Nobody has actually said that he saw M. dead. Nobody claims ever to have washed his body and put it in the grave. For those who went through the camps, life was like a delirium in which the sequence of time was lost and fact was mixed with fantasy . . . I can be certain of only one thing: that somewhere M.'s sufferings ended in death. Before that he must have lain dying on his bunk like others around him . . . And after his death – or even before it, perhaps – he lived on in camp legend as a demented old man of seventy who had once written poetry in the outside world . . . And another old man – or was it the same one? – lived in the transit camp at Vtorya Rechka, waiting to be shipped to Kolyma, and was thought by many people to be Osip Mandelstam – which, for all I know, he may have been.

The reference in that passage to Mandelstam's age as 'seventy' derives from the recollection of another prisoner who had seen him at an earlier stage of his incarceration, and who had assumed from his appearance that that was his age. (He was actually in his late forties then.) The whole passage is not only intensely moving; it also illustrates one of the central ideas which inform the book as a whole. A few paragraphs earlier I referred to the author's capacity for justifying, in action as it were, the general reflections she offers to the reader. In fact, she does much more than this with them. Her ideas are not used in order to abstract herself from her experience but only as a way of getting more closely to grips with it; they are an expression of her determination to master what she has been through, to draw conclusions from it which other people would feel to be as true for themselves and for other times as they are for herself and her own era. The result is that her generalisations and speculations are ultimately inseparable from the restraint and stoicism she shows in describing the events in which she was a participant, or from the zest for life which she reveals even under the most arduous conditions, or from her wit, or from the sharpness with which she draws portraits of individual Russians, famous and unknown, or from her unflinching zeal simply to put down her story, complete, regardless of what the authorities might exact from her in retribution for what she has done. Her ideas, in other words, are organic to the book: as much a saving presence in it as we feel them to have been in her life.

*

The central idea which the book articulates and exemplifies is that of an ineluctable human continuity, for good and evil, informing everything we do and are, whether in times of mortal crisis or in the give and take of everyday existence – or, indeed, in the everydayness of times of crisis, too. The way in which we are told of Mandelstam's anonymous martyrdom in Siberia, one man among others, each of whom is as individual and as indistinguishable as himself, is just one example of how her understanding of the continuity we have with one another animates the book. The author does not so much perceive it in her vision of her husband's death; she uses it as her faculty of perception.

There are many other passages in the book about which the same could be said. I have never read a more vivid account of what it is like to live for month after month, and year after year, under a reign of terror; but then I have never read anything which showed so deep a comprehension of how the terror creates an unbreakable bond between the murderers and their victims. It does so by implicating everyone, without exception, in its operations – through fear, suspicion, bribes, secrecy, lies, grotesque confessions, a crazy arbitrariness in the selection of prisoners, the sheer number of arrests – so that in the end there is no one who can feel himself to be wholly innocent, whether before the regime itself, before his family and friends, or before his own conscience. The result? 'We all took the easy way out, in the hope that not we but our neighbours would be killed . . . Crushed by the system each of us had in some way or other helped to build, we were not even capable of passive resistance.'

Because she spares herself and even Mandelstam so little, she establishes a continuity of another kind between her readers and the people she is writing about. She describes how she lived, and how her husband was dragged to his death, in one of the greatest cataclysms to overcome any people in a century of cataclysms; but for the unscathed reader in the West she also creates at every point a sense of perfect congruence between himself and the human motives and responses presented on her pages. At every page we turn, in every story she tells of human nature put under almost unparalleled stress, we are compelled to recognise ourselves. And not just our imagined selves, either, the selves we might have been, but those we are now, today: at school, at work, at home, in the bus queue, anywhere and all the time.

The author also explores the connection between what she sees as the prior corruption of the intellectuals and the reign of terror that was to destroy perhaps more members of the intelligentsia, proportionately, than of any other class. She does not hold the intelligentsia directly responsible for the terror; but she does accuse her fellow intellectuals of having made its triumph more certain. By attempting to overthrow traditional moral values, initially perhaps out of a hatred of hypocrisy, but also because they revelled in the sheer excitement of dismantling what had been passed on to them; by finding so glamorous the idea of an all-cleansing, all-renewing revolution as to be unable to separate themselves from any of its manifestations; by despising the present in which they lived in favour of a more splendid future they confidently looked to history to bring about; and by combining all this with common careerism, power-worship, and a desire to run with the pack, the intellectuals helped to bring about their own destruction and that of their fellow citizens.

How, in the author's view, could it be otherwise? What is the lure of an all-embracing revolutionary ideology if not the promise that the continuities which have bound people to one another in families and societies, and across generations, are of no consequence, or are nothing more than a source of oppression? But when those bonds are scorned and disrupted, they do not disappear; instead they return in forms more malign than any we could have dreamed of before.

The direct continuity of art with life – hardly a fashionable belief in the West today – is taken for granted by the author. Her description of Mandelstam's methods of composition has great inwardness and understanding; it is also marked by its modesty, for she makes no claim for herself as anything but his scribe and the protector of his manuscripts from the vengeance of the authorities. From her account of it, the writing of poems seems to have been for him as much a physical as a mental activity; he spoke of it as a 'ringing in his ears', a 'movement of his lips', a 'wearing out of shoe leather'. But he and she, for all the vagrancy of their life together, obviously had a deep impulse to cherish the natural world and the ordinarily changeableness of daily life. ('A plant is an event, an occurrence, an arrow,' she quotes him as saying with characteristic, heretical recklessness, 'not a boring *development* with a beard.') Her ever-present sense of the dependence of one human fact on every other often leads her to speak pessimistically about the future of her country, which has committed such crimes against itself that she finds it difficult to imagine how it might ever recover. But she also occasionally writes with rather more optimism of the chances of a people learning from its past, and of culture as 'not something generated by the upper layer of a society at any given time [it is the upper layer of Soviet society that she has in mind here], but . . . a product of the continuity without which life would break into chaos.'

That is one of the few places in the book where the author actually uses the word which I have described here as central to her understanding of what she went through. Perhaps the best way of indicating the warmth of her book is to say that the central image of continuity, of mutual human dependence, which it presents to us is simply that of a marriage, of a man and a woman in a room together. In many chapters the reader has a strange impression that he is hearing two voices, not one, as the author recalls her husband's questions or observations or jokes – or his passing infatuations with other women – and adds her comments and replies, some made then, some in the very act of writing. We feel at such moments that we are listening to a marital conversation which in a sense is still continuing, though time and terror have done their worst.

During the years that have passed since their first appearance in the West, Nadezhda Mandelstam's two volumes have been circulated in the Soviet Union only in *samizdat* form. Stalin's body may have been removed from the place it originally occupied in the Kremlin wall, his statue may have vanished from all the public squares which it once disfigured (leaving only the bald head and mountebank beard of Lenin universally on display), his name may have been banished from people's lips; but such enforced emptyings and silences, such zealous pretendings-it-never-happened, are in themselves nothing more than a Stalinist way of dealing with the horrors of the past. Today as in the past those who rule the country are incapable of claiming for themselves any legitimacy other than that which comes to them, ideologically and institutionally, through the Stalin regime and hence through the crimes of that era. Mandelstam, they are prepared to say, was the victim of an 'error', of an 'excess'. His wife's memoirs tell us what such words mean. No wonder the rulers of the Soviet Union do not want their own people to hear her.

ELEVEN

SINYAVSKY'S ART

LILITH: I think there is more sorrow in the world
Than man can bear.

NUBIAN: None can exceed their limit, lady:
You either bear or break.

– Isaac Rosenberg, *The Amulet*

Our consciousness fills up all the space available to it with whatever materials are to hand. It cannot do otherwise. If circumstances proffer it peace, comfort, the ordinary chances of domestic existence, then it will make its world of these. If you have small grievances they will occupy the entire 'grievance space' within you, however contracted or expansive that space might happen to be. With ambitions, likewise. Fears, too. The mayor of a small town taking the oath of office for the first time feels himself at one with the great figures of the world, almost a presence in history. His son, sitting at midnight in the only eating place in town which is open at that hour, sees himself as a desperado, a night owl, a man without illusions. The *bien pensant* intellectual in the metropolis feels the panic of isolation and exposure at the very thought of being out of step with his fellows on any important issue. The child who puts on a new pair of shoes is so bedazzled by their shine he imagines everyone in the street to be looking at him. These examples have not been chosen simply in order to be ridiculed. On the contrary. Which of us does not remember the shames and excitements of childhood as the most intense of our lives, though the occasion for them may now seem to us trivial or absurd?

But what if the circumstances we know suddenly undergo a wholesale transformation? If the world proves itself to be quite other than the place we had previously imagined it to be? If fate or our own choice or some unfathomable

83

mixture of both plunges us suddenly into a wholly different context, into a war, a natural catastrophe, a prison? Or into a hospital?

> What is so disconcerting is not so much this other reality in itself, as the mere possibility of its being so near that you only have to make one step to cross over into a new existence just as self-contained and valid as the previous one; and thus find the thought of a plurality of worlds confirmed with a terrifying suddenness.

That passage was written by Andrey Sinyavsky (Abram Tertz) in a letter to his wife, while serving a seven-year sentence in a prison camp for 'slandering the Soviet Union' – i.e. for publishing his works abroad without government permission. Ironically enough, he is referring here not to his confinement in prison, but to his transfer from the prison camp to a hospital, after serving the first five years of his sentence. The key word in the passage, it seems to me, is *valid*: in his use of it there lies at least a hint of why some people are able to 'bear', in Rosenberg's phrase, while others 'break'. Or, if everybody breaks should sufficient pressure be put on them for long enough, why some people do so sooner than others. To try to accept the validity, the thereness, the truth of this new reality, and to use it as the material for a new consciousness, to fill your imagination with the circumstances into which you have been thrust in a moment of revolutionary change, can be not natural or inevitable at all, but an act of great moral fortitude. 'From the moment you go to prison,' Solzhenitsyn writes in the first volume of *The Gulag Archipelago*, after describing how he himself had responded to the shock of his arrest by trying desperately to cling to his status as an officer in the Soviet army, 'you must put your cosy past firmly behind you. You must say to yourself: "I no longer have any property whatever. For me those I love have died, and for them I have died."'

The paradox, it would seem, is that if you are indeed able to bid farewell to your past entitlements and expectations, you may be able to retain a genuine continuity with the person you were before; whereas to see the new life only as a personal affront, an imposition, an uncalled-for misfortune and an act of grotesque injustice (even if, or especially if, it is indeed an act of injustice) – that in fact may be to 'break', to cease to be. Which goes some way, perhaps, to explaining why Rosenberg could write with such stoicism out of the trenches of the First World War, and why Sinyavsky/Tertz can say wearily a few pages later in *A Voice from the Chorus*, the book put together from his prison letters:

> Notions like 'human dignity' or 'the inviolability of the person' are to my mind a kind of gobbledegook, part of a generally accepted jargon or code serving the same sort of practical convenience as exclamatory phrases such as 'you don't say!' or 'goodness gracious' – which are all very well in polite conversation, but make little real sense and cannot be taken very seriously. At bottom there is no

such thing as 'personal dignity'. In some book or other great indignation is expressed at the fact that Plato was sold into slavery. Plato – into slavery? But why not? What more suited to Plato?

That last remark, it should be said, is anything but an expression of some personal or philosophical antipathy to Plato. The argument is, rather, that Plato can only truly be taken to be an example of the highest form of a certain kind of human development if he has also experienced the most intense forms of human adversity. To believe in 'human dignity' while sitting in a comfortable armchair, and in 'the inviolability of the person' after a very good meal, requires no special effort. But the discarding of such beliefs can be the first step towards being able to see more clearly and to accept more fully what one has become.

*

When he went into prison Andrey Sinyavsky was known in the West (under the Tertz pseudonym) as the author of a series of fantastic novellas, *The Trial Begins, The Icicle,* and *The Makepeace Experiment.* None of these works had been published in the author's native country, where they had been seen by the authorities as both a direct and indirect challenge to themselves. They were a direct challenge because they dealt in a contemptuous manner with the minds, personalities, and motives of the state's highest and lowest functionaries alike, and took for granted the moral corruptions and absurdities at the heart of the system. They were an indirect challenge because nothing could have been further from the state-approved doctrines of 'socialist realism' than Sinyavsky's fantastic and playful mode of writing. In his stories and novels he had set his own comedy of paranoia and obsession against the paranoias and obsessions of those who ran the state and all its organs; he had held up to ridicule the authorities' attempt at securing an ultimate or total control over the citizens of their state by comparing it with the mastery a novelist has over the fate of his characters.

In one of the best stories in *The Icicle,* for example, the chief character is driven crazy by his belief that he is being pursued everywhere by the secret police, little knowing that the omnipresent power which is keeping him under surveillance is merely that of the novelist himself. In the title story of the same collection a young man is endowed miraculously, and to his own torment, with second sight: not only can he see what is going to happen in this life to the people around him, he can also see what happened to them aeons before in previous incarnations, and what will happen to them aeons hence in incarnations yet to come. Naturally, on hearing of his possession of these powers, the authorities wish to harness him and them to their political needs, internally and externally. In *The Makepeace Experiment* another young man, getting hold of a book with a certain resemblance, as a holy text, to *Das Kapital,* develops uncanny powers over physical matter and people's perceptions, and uses these to set up an autonomous republic in a provincial town.

Sinyavsky's fiction belongs, then, to that strain of fantasy in the Russian tradition which runs from Gogol through the Dostoevsky of a novel like *The Double* or a short story like 'The Crocodile', towards such twentieth century writers as Mikhail Bulgakov and Vladimir Nabokov. The influence of Dostoevsky is felt most strongly perhaps in the desperate, deadpan courtesy with which Sinyavsky's characters seek to confront wholly unprecedented and unlikely situations. 'Forgive me . . .,' says the scribe of *The Makepeace Experiment*, addressing an intrusive, ghostly presence from his childhood, 'shouldn't you be dead by rights, if you'll excuse my saying so?' An English reader may also wonder, incidentally, whether or not Sinyavsky had read and admired *Tristram Shandy*, for some of the tricks he gets up to are very similar to Sterne's: especially that of 'estranging' the reader by reminding him of the book in his hand as a physical object. In *The Makepeace Experiment*, for instance, there are a series of running footnotes, which are inserted in the text against the narrator's will, and which he refers to as the 'cellars' or 'vaults' of the book.

Even from this brief account of it, it should be clear that Sinyavsky's fantasy is so thoroughgoing, so subversive of everyday reality and the terms in which we usually try to comprehend it, that one should not fall into the Soviet trap of regarding his writing purely as a kind of covert politics. The political intentions of his tales are indistinguishable from their specifically literary ambitions and curiosities, and from a sense of unbounded human and non-human possibility which the author delights both in contemplating and teasing us with. *The Icicle* is alive with the author's wonder at the transience of our physical forms and the permanence of our hungers, and with his bafflement at the fact that creatures as solitary as ourselves should also be as intertwined with one another as we are.

One of the problems with fantasy as a fictional mode, however, is that it is always in danger of degenerating into mere whimsy. Only a firm internal logic generated from within, a strict attention to the rules which the story sets itself as it unfolds, is likely to avert that danger. The logic of Kafka's *The Metamorphosis* is all but remorseless; hence the comedy and the pathos, even the tragedy, of the tale. The same could be said about the first two episodes of *Gulliver's Travels*, though the effects Swift is aiming at are of a very different kind; or, for that matter, about something like H.G. Wells's *The Island of Doctor Moreau*. With Marquez's *A Hundred Years of Solitude*, on the other hand, or Kundera's *The Unbearable Lightness of Being*, the longer we go on reading the more we come to feel that the author has so contrived things that he can say more or less what he likes at any point, and can arrange for almost anything to happen next. Then we get what seems to me the worst of both worlds: laborious whimsy, plodding whimsy. If Sinyavsky usually manages to escape this fate it is not because we are always confident that he knows how to develop dramatically the situations he has created. It is rather because he has the artistic tact to keep his inventions swift, short, seemingly offhand, deliberately underplayed.

*

Nothing in Sinyavsky's impudently freakish fictions could ultimately be as bizarre as the fact that he was sentenced to seven years' hard labour for the 'crime' of writing them and of then succeeding in getting them published abroad. (It was because it was so dangerous to publish his work abroad without prior authorisation that he had adopted a self-protective pseudonym at the beginning of his career.) *A Voice from the Chorus* is the book that emerged from those years in a labour-camp. It is his prison-book, just as (to name only a few) Yevgenia Ginsburg's *Into the Whirlwind* was hers, and Anatoly Marchenko's *My Testimony*, and Edward Kuznetsov's *Prison Diaries*, and Andrei Amalric's *Involuntary Journey to Siberia*, and Menachem Begin's *White Nights* were theirs. (Yes, that is the Begin who later became Prime Minister of Israel; and an alert, open, and surprisingly good humoured book his turns out to be, once the first couple of bombastic chapters about his interrogation have been left behind.) Each of these accounts of life in Soviet labour camps from the 1930s onwards is impressive in its own way; all, like Sinyavsky's own, one has to add, are overshadowed by Solzhenitsyn's stupendous achievement in *The Gulag Archipelago*.*

One point to be made about that achievement is particularly relevant here. Among so much else that Solzhenitsyn managed to do in *The Gulag Archipelago* is to invent a new literary form: an observation which may seem trivial enough in view of the scope of his subject and the sheer horror it encompasses. But I think it worth saying, because what Solzhenitsyn has to tell us is in a strict sense inseparable from the mode in which it is told. The alternation he makes between autobiography and general history throughout the three volumes, chapter by chapter, section upon section, is something that to my knowledge has never been done before; certainly not on anything approaching this scale.

To have reconstructed the unrecorded, forbidden past of an entire generation, to have excavated singlehandedly one of the two greatest crimes of the century, would have been an astonishing feat. So would it have been to have given, with so much insight and boisterous rage, the account of his arrest, his prisons, his camps, his trains, his gaolers, his fellow-prisoners, his survival. But to have done both, to have brought the two together and to have maintained an equilibrium between them, so that each part makes the other starker, clearer, more veracious, is an accomplishment quite without precedent. So far as it is possible for us to be made to believe a story as terrible as the one told in *The Gulag Archipelago*, we are brought to do so because each of the narratives of which it is composed, the individual and the general, the autobiographical and the historical, contains or implies the other. The autobiography, in other words, manages to be as 'impersonal' as the history, and the history is felt as intimately as the

---

* Lucky the country without a copious prison literature. It is hardly surprising that some of the strongest writing to have come out of South Africa over the last decade has taken the form of prison memoirs. I am thinking especially of Hugh Lewin's *Bandiet: Seven Years in a South African Prison* and Breyten Breytenbach's *Confessions of an Albino Terrorist*.

autobiography. It is in these volumes that Solzhenitsyn's attachment to the Tolstoy of *War and Peace*, which is so evident in *The First Circle* and *August 1914*, justifies itself completely.

The contrast with Sinyavsky/Tertz's *A Voice from the Chorus* is extreme. (Except in one regard, to which I shall return.) Even the fact that the book carries both the author's real name and his pseudonym on its covers, though he was living in the West when it was published and was thus safe from the vengeance of the Soviet authorities, is an instance of the indirection of his literary method. The book is made up, as I have said, of passages from letters to his wife, together with some brief diary entries composed after his release. The physical circumstances of his incarceration hardly appear in it. Unlike every other author mentioned above, he tells us absolutely nothing about his arrest, the reasons given for his imprisonment, the course of his trial. Apart from the occasional description of an exchanged glance or some other particularly striking encounter, his fellow-prisoners are present only through a series of italicised and unexplained quotations of remarks overheard ('The Chorus'). These anonymous quotations are all brief, some consisting of just a few words; but the anthologies of them which punctuate the text sometimes extend over several pages. Fragments of dialogue, boasts about past misdeeds, malapropisms, idle conjectures about the future or the meaning of life, fantasies about sex or money – the author obviously treasured some for their bizarre power and originality, others for their excruciating banality.

At one point in his communings with himself or his wife, he points out that a line of verse consists 'not only of [its] alternation of sounds, but even more the organisation of pauses, the arrangement of silences and stillnesses.' This remark can be extended to apply to the book as a whole. His extreme frugality in speaking of the conditions in which he is writing, and his total abstention of any discussion of what had brought him there, have a double effect. They put into particularly sharp focus those sudden details of his daily existence which do appear, and they lend an extraordinary deliberateness and intensity to the reflections on other topics of which the book is largely composed. We become aware, for example, of the relentless, tormenting gregariousness of camp life through his quiet remark on how difficult he finds it to read a letter from his son when so many eyes are on him; or through the wonder he expresses at the way in which the prisoners playing dominoes *always* have to shout out exactly the same things whenever they put down their pieces. The shaving of his head is mentioned explicitly only because it makes his head ache each time; when he hangs a new towel above his bed 'it was almost the equivalent of a spring cleaning.'

For the rest, intertwined naturally with such moments, and echoing or contradicting the utterances of the inane, savage, ramblingly philosophical chorus ('Ah well, life's just a transit camp'; or 'Your cock is still crowing in your pants': or 'In Leningrad all the houses are architectural!') – intertwined with such moments are aphorisms, *pensées* about art and history, recollections of childhood, passages of descriptive writing about natural phenomena, brief essays on works of literature like *Hamlet* or *Robinson Crusoe*, analyses of myths and items of folklore. Again and again as one reads the serene, poignant paragraphs and little essays on topics such as these, one finds oneself thinking, 'To have written like that – there!' But each time the entire book seems to re-form itself in one's mind as a quiet reminder or rebuke, and one remembers the remark about Plato which I quoted above. To be what it is, it had to be written – just there.

A Voice from the Chorus succeeds wholly in making apparent the inner logic and force of its own surprising form. But an interesting view of it, and of Sinyavsky/Tertz's earlier work, is to be gained from a long essay, entitled 'The Literary Process in Russia', which the author published in the emigré journal, *Kontinent*. In this essay, as might be expected, he declares his opposition to 'realism' as a literary mode or doctrine. What is less predictable is that he has in mind here not the realism of official Soviet literature, which he regards as being quite beneath notice, but that of his fellow-dissident or *samizdat* writers. The danger facing *samizdat*, he says, is that it will assume 'the role of a sort of whining complaints book, supposedly to be perused by the leaders (who don't give a damn anyway), or to be stored away in a cupboard until the advent of those better times when people will have learned to live by the light of truth . . . [It] will again be reduced to a recital of the torments we suffer and the remedies we offer to put in its place . . . We must put a stop to cringing and currying favour with the hectoring taskmaster – reality! After all, we *are* writers, artists in words.' He then goes on to plead with his fellow writers to create instead 'on this fertile, well-manured soil [of Russia] . . . something astonishing, something exotic.'

Ironically enough, *A Voice from the Chorus* comes closer than Sinyavsky's fiction has so far done to fulfilling wholly the aims outlined in the article just quoted. It is in this respect, I think, that it can be fairly compared to *The Gulag Archipelago*. There we have a case of a novelist finding in a documentary work the fullest possible expression of his imaginative and rhetorical powers. Sinyavsky's prison book is also eager to take into itself as much as it can of the hateful reality he was compelled to experience. But he will permit it to do so only on his own imperious and ingenious terms; only through the exercise of an abstemiousness which teases the reader's expectations and turns its back with a quiet deliberation – even here; especially here – on the regime that incarcerated him. The result is that he has succeeded in producing what he has asked for from others: an exotic and astonishing work.

PART FOUR

LAWRENCIAN

TWELVE

WOMEN IN LOVE AND THE DEATH OF THE WILL

———◆———

Lawrence's theory of the individual psyche was inseparable, on the one side, from elaborate notions or fantasies about human physiology, in which words like 'ganglia' and 'solar plexus' figured prominently. On the other side, this theory was attached directly to his beliefs about society in general and the forces animating nothing less than the universe as a whole. Just as it was impossible for him to talk about mind without talking about body, too, for their unity seemed manifest to him, a given of his experience, so it was impossible for him to consider the relations between men and women, or between the citizen and the community, without invoking sanctions which he believed to be ultimately religious in character. His detestation of industrial society sprang in large measure from his conviction that it was set upon wresting for the human race an independence from the natural order which it had never had and never could have. The modern world, as he saw it, encouraged men and women to find meaning and satisfaction in their lives as producers and consumers of material goods, as members of competing political parties or nation-states, as manipulators of yet more and more powerful machines, instead of as creatures whose ultimate allegiance should always be to powers beyond themselves.

How, then, was the individual psyche structured and how did it function or fall into malfunction? With remarkable consistency from book to book, Lawrence argued that within each individual there is to be found a 'dark self' (or 'blood being' or 'blood consciousness' or 'active unconsciousness') which is closely though never wholly identified with the body, and which exists independently of, and anterior to, 'the ordinary mental consciousness' (or 'white self' or 'social ego' or 'personality' or 'mental-subjective self'). As readers will know, he offered a number of other, parallel terms for those mentioned in the last sentence. When the psyche is healthy, the dark self, which is the true source of the passions and the true centre of response to the outside world, has primacy and power over the mental consciousness, which should properly do no more than translate the 'creative flux' of life into the 'shorthand' of ideas, abstractions, principles, and ideals.

When the relationship of forces within the individual has been disturbed, however, the mental consciousness, with its ideas and ideals, usurps the primacy which should belong to the dark self; it comes between the individual and whatever is outside him or is unknown to him, and determines *a priori* what his response shall be; it repudiates the life of the body and the senses and – using the will as its executive arm, so to speak – seeks to impose upon the self and the world the fixed, static abstractions which are all that it can ever know and contain. Instead of being open and receptive, aware always of the 'otherness' of fellow humans and animals, and of the universe they inhabit, the individual becomes a creature of his or her own fixed will: self-enclosed, self-referring, insentient. Such people have in effect willed themselves into a condition resembling that of an automaton; but by the same token the will in each of them has itself become an automatism, a machine.

Given the unifying tendencies of Lawrence's modes of thought and perception, it is hardly surprising that he should have regarded the affinity between the 'machine' of the runaway will and the machines of the industrial world as more than a metaphorical one. An individual who has degenerated in the manner just described, who has to all intents turned himself into a machine, is bound to see society, the natural world, and indeed his own innermost being, as fields for the exercise of his will, instead of as the unpredictable, 'spontaneous-creative' welter of contending forces they actually are. But once the industrial system exists out there, anyway, it in turn forces into its own shape the psyches of those who live within it. The community ceases to exist and becomes instead an agglomeration of so many enclosed egos, each convinced of its own importance and yet all subject to the whims, hysterias, and fixed ideas of the others.

For these reasons Lawrence was inclined to direct his wrath most fiercely against just those social and moral ambitions – or achievements – which have generally been regarded as some measure of compensation for the dangers and disorders of technological development. He regarded the modern passion for equality and social justice – itself ultimately dependent on a wide diffusion of material wealth – as evil and misdirected; the modern hankering for physical comfort and security as a corruption; the notion of the importance, indeed the sanctity, of the individual personality as a tyranny and disease. It was not the failure (in so many places, at so many times) of the industrial society to achieve its own ambitions that infuriated him, as we can perhaps say about someone like Dickens in *Hard Times*; it was the attempt itself. For example:

The ideal of love, the ideal that it is better to give than to receive, the ideal of liberty, the ideal of the brotherhood of man, the ideal of the sanctity of human life, the ideal of what we call goodness, charity, benevolence, public spiritedness, the ideal of sacrifice for a cause, the ideal of unity and unanimity – all the lot – the whole beehive of ideals – has all got the modern bee-disease, and gone putrid, stinking. And when the ideal is dead and putrid, the logical consequence is only stink. Which, for me, is the truth concerning the ideal of good, peaceful, loving humanity and its logical consequence in Socialism and equality, equal opportunity or whatever you like. By this time he stinketh – and I'm sorry for any Christus who brings him to life again, to stink livingly for another thirty years: the beastly Lazarus of our idealism.

The passage comes from *Aaron's Rod*, from a speech by Lilley, who is plainly the voice and presence of Lawrence in the novel. Any reader will know that it can be paralleled by scores of similar outbursts from the works which immediately preceded and followed *Aaron's Rod*, and from the letters of the period.

This is the state, Lawrence insists, to which we have been brought by 'the human idealism which governs us now so ruthlessly and vilely'; and to which he sees the liberal, the capitalist, the Communist, and the Christian all equally committed. 'What tyranny', he asks, 'is so hideous as that of an *automatically ideal humanity?*' (My italics.) Much the most powerful of the abstractions which he believed to have become fixed into a series of irresistible mental injunctions were those drawn from centuries of propagation of Christianity, and the secular gospels of love and social welfare which were derived in one form or another from Christianity. It was against the gospel of love that he reacted most fiercely: against love in its religious forms; love in the ordinary sexual meaning of the word; and love in its modern, material manifestations, in what he called 'the industrial-lovey-dovey-darling-take-me-to-mamma state of things'. All these, equally, were in his view expressions of the imperialistic, conscious, ideal-mongering will which ruled us and by which we sought to rule each other and the world at large.

It may well seem odd to us that a writer whose most productive years coincided more or less with the First World War, the Communist revolution, and the economic crises which racked the subsequent decade, and who died shortly before Hitler came to power in Germany, should condemn his society for being 'lovey-dovey' rather than for being cruel and rapacious. But in fact Lawrence was ready to blame the lovey-dovey idealists of every hue for being savagely, though secretly, bloodthirsty as well. Beneath the tyranny of an insensate 'automatic idealism', the raped and despoiled dark self suffered and sought its revenge; those who claimed to uphold the conscious ideals which the society set before itself were filled with an unadmitted craving for destruction and anarchy, and had done and would continue to do their utmost to bring the world to ruin.

*

The novel in which Lawrence seeks most closely to anatomise this diseased and aberrant will, as he saw it, is *Women in Love*. Not that the subject disappears from his fiction after the publication of that novel; far from it. But in many of the novels and stories which followed he seems to have taken his own diagnosis as in a sense proven: what he did subsequently was to re-state it, to re-examine it, to dramatise it in different forms, to give it wholly different contexts geographically and even spiritually. Thus *Kangaroo*, his Australian novel, is primarily political in focus; *The Plumed Serpent*, its Mexican counterpart, religious; *Lady Chatterley's Lover*, needless to say, sexual. In none of these, though, are quite so many different *kinds* of characters revealed so insistently to be suffering from quite so many manifestations of that fatal hypertrophy of the same organ or faculty as in *Women in Love*. Reading the book one cannot help being reminded sometimes of the closing episodes of Proust's *Remembrance of Things Past*, in which the characters successively doff their masks and reveal themselves to the reader and to one another as homosexuals.

Hermione, Gerald, and Gudrun, as well as Thomas Crich and Loerke, among the more important characters, and such minor figures as Diana Crich, who kills the young man who tries to save her from drowning, Minette the *demi-mondaine* (whose will it is to submit), and Palmer, the young electrical engineer with whom Gudrun has a brief relationship, not to mention those ashen-faced, anonymous miners and townsfolk who 'had a secret sense of power, and of inexpressible destructiveness, and of fatal half-heartedness, a sort of rottenness in the will' – all are afflicted in one fashion or another with the disease. Therefore they are all to be seen as death-seekers and death-dealers: so much the more empoisoned in themselves and poisonous to others because they believe they are serving noble causes, or are at least engaged in activities greater than themselves. Gudrun and Loerke are artists; Thomas Crich is a philanthropist who has the welfare of the downtrodden at heart; Gerald, the industrial magnate, tries through his machines to serve the greatest good of the greatest number; Hermione devotes herself in her own way to the intellectual life. But the one activity to which they are all committed in their hearts is that of destruction.

Even Ursula and Birkin, the 'good' characters, it is worth noting, constantly accuse each other of being bossy and dictatorial and wilful; but, fortunately for them, a kind of divine election (i.e. the author's predetermining of the matter) never stops working in their favour. They are both entitled to speak with great longing, as the other characters never do, of the destruction of the entire human race, and of how blessed the world would be once it is rid of humanity. None of this, however, leads to their being accused by the narrative voice or by the other characters of manifesting therefore a murderously diseased will. The others, by contrast, can barely say or do anything – make love, give to charity, paint, teach, talk – without revealing or being said to reveal how advanced, how gangrenous, their condition really is.

But then, Lawrence would have us believe it is precisely Ursula and Birkin's readiness to acknowledge their own distaste for the human race and their longing for its quiet extinction, in their more despairing moods, that differentiates their condition from that of the others, whose destructive urges are so deep and so well-concealed they hardly ever become aware of them.

*

Qui s'excuse, s'accuse goes the old saying. In Lawrence's case, *qui accuse les autres, se révèle.* He was prone from the very beginning of his career to deal with his neurasthenic obsessions by diagnosing them as the ills of *others*: we can already clearly see the process at work in *Sons and Lovers*, where the author never sides so closely with Paul Morel as when he is acccusing poor Miriam of an excessive intensity of feeling together with an excessive sexual timidity. We see it again, in a markedly different form, in his letters after he and Frieda had fled from England, when he repeatedly and loudly proclaimed the hateful 'deadness' of the country he had left behind: the country, that is, in which his beloved mother had recently died and he himself had suffered from an almost fatal crisis immediately afterwards, and from which there came an incessant series of tormented and tormenting letters from Frieda's distraught husband.

The case of *Women in Love* is both different and similar once again. Critics usually write as if the chief problem for the reader with the novel, as with the rest of Lawrence's later fiction, is that of coming to terms with the constant jar between the author's doctrinal prepossessions and the novelistic and dramatic action within the books. They defend the novels (when they defend them) by insisting that the doctrine never takes over completely; that what the characters say and do and feel is never wholly reducible to the lessons which Lawrence the preacher and theorist would have us draw from them; that the dramatic and descriptive patterns to be discerned in the books escape from and in some cases actually controvert 'the message'. All this is true, so far as it goes; yet I would argue that to speak of *Women in Love*, at least, in such terms is in effect to evade the depth at which the doctrine works in the novel and its strange, self-subversive manner of making itself felt dramatically.

The point is this. The critics write as if there is a direct contrast or cleavage between, on the one hand, that which is active and unstable and changeable in the book – what the characters do and perceive, the relationships they have with one another, and their experience of the natural world – and, on the other hand, Lawrence's doctrinal preoccupations. The former elements are obviously felt to be capable of unexpected and even self-contradictory development; the latter, by and large, are regarded as fixed and hence as inherently undramatic. To use two well-known images from Lawrence's own criticism: they are the novelist's 'thumb in the pan' or the 'nail' that tries to pin the characters down and hold them fast within a particular moral scheme. What else can the doctrine be and how else can it work, critics generally seem to suppose, if it is possible to abstract it from the novel as I tried to do at the beginning of this essay, or if Lawrence himself could develop it in a more or less continuous fashion in books different even in genre from *Women in Love*? For doctrine to *be* doctrine it has surely to be something detachable from its context, not dependent for its life (as the characters undoubtedly are) on the sway of impulse and action in the narrative.

The truth, though, is that it is not only the characters who can outflank and outwit and contradict their creator; the doctrine itself can do so too, once it is let loose in a novel. It too can become a source of drama and self-contradiction and inadvertent self-revelation; it too, to quote one of the essays by Lawrence to which I referred in the previous paragraph, is capable of surprising the novelist by 'getting up and walking away with the nail'. *Women in Love* presents itself as an anatomy of that diseased and hyperactive will which Lawrence believes is going to put paid – and pretty soon too – to our civilisation as a whole. The deepest irony of the book, however, is that there can be few English novels comparable with it in scope and ambition in which we feel the will of the author to be so unremittingly and implacably at work, on every level, as we do in reading this one.

Of course, no novel is ever written involuntarily; all are expressions, in a sense, of the author's will. But we recognise readily enough the operation of that creative will which is capable of being so completely absorbed in the task which it has set itself as to vanish not just from our awareness but, it would seem, from that of the novelist as well. As it happens, Lawrence himself is a writer (even in *Women in Love* at times, and in innumerable places outside it) of whom this can be said with a particular appropriateness. At his best he writes like a supernaturally gifted sportsman making his strokes: there appears to be no gap whatever between eye, brain, and hand; the words just seem to *happen* on the page rather than to have arrived there as the result of any conceivable process of calculation or volition. The sporting analogy I have just drawn is obviously inadequate in at least one important respect: often enough, what this brain and eye were observing, and this hand was transcribing, was not so much external 'events' as internal states and feelings. Yet the effect is the same: the observation and the act of communicating it are perfectly integrated with one another and the writer has total, impersonal confidence in both. Hence the dazzling swiftness and spontaneity of which he is capable, and the effortless transitions between (or combinations of) wit and passion, dramatic action and dramatic stillness, which the writing manages to achieve.

By contrast, we can recognise too the presence in what we read of that authorial will which proclaims itself, as it were, on the page; which draws attention to itself; which does not let either the reader or the characters in its created world escape from its presence. It is an assertive will of the latter kind, I suggest, which we feel to be at work in most of *Women in Love*. From its very first page we are aware of the unflagging determination of the author to make something of this novel that would be different from anything that had gone before: to find a way of presenting characters and their relationships with one another which would be unprecedented; to develop a psychic-physical notation unlike any other to convey their inner life (hence all those swoons, electric shocks, dimmings of the mind, faintings of the blood, voluptuous shudderings, and the rest, which the characters feel in one another's company) – and to use all this, and more besides, to compel the reader's emotions and reflections to go the way he wanted.

Yes, Lawrence was striving for a genuine originality of approach to character and narrative in the book; and for that he is not to be reproached. That was his intention, and in varying measure it was his achievement too. But intentions and the effects mentioned above are not separable in any way from what we feel to be the determination of the author to hunt down certain characters and to convict them of a worse-than-criminal guilt in their dealings with one another and with mankind in general. Nor are those intentions and achievements separable from his determination that certain other characters, as we have seen, should be judged essentially blameless whatever they say or feel about those around them. Nor are the ambitions of the novel to be separated from its sheer, unending, exhausting *talkiness*: the way in which everything that happens in it becomes a topic for conversational analysis at the first opportunity, and thus another element in the authorial campaign relentlessly pushing the reader towards conclusions – which are also premises. (Though this last aspect of the book does not prevent Hermione being condemned smartly because, if you please, she *'loves* discussion' . . .). Much the same can be said about the random, offhand sowing of death among the ranks of the Crich family. After all, why should they not go, one after the other, when the last of the conclusions to which the novel remorselessly yet wearily pushes itself, as Birkin and Ursula are allowed to acknowledge, is that longed-for annulment of the will which only death – everyone's death, universal death – can bring?

And all this, mark you, in a novel which tells us over and over again that the sickness to death which ravages us, and from which only a few are uncertainly or provisionally spared, is an excess of will! What the novel would like to set before us as an alternative to a life governed by the will is one in which the will is laid asleep: 'so that that which is perfectly ourselves can take place in us'. Sometimes we are told that we may know this condition only when the world has at last been cleansed of us as we now are, and the new start has become possible; intermittently, in fleeting moments, we are shown what this state might be like in the here and now. One such moment is that in which Gerald and Gudrun float peacefully together in the boat, just before the terrible screams are heard that accompany his sister's drowning; another is the meeting between Birkin and Ursula after she has had a pitiful, commonplace row with her father.

More often, though, what the novel most vividly illustrates is a condition so much at odds with itself as to be almost beyond the reach of language: an irresistible, at times quite uncontrollable, will-to-death that springs from the novelist's hatred and weariness of the will.

THIRTEEN

ALPHA AND OMEGA

———◆———

D.H. Lawrence on the Revelation which was vouchsafed to the biblical John of Patmos? Those who know both writers might well be inclined to fear the worst. Woozy metaphysics. Wild history. Bloodstained theology. Vituperation galore. Promises of chaos to come. Even more dismaying glimpses of redemption to follow. Etcetera.

Well, one does find something of these in Lawrence's *Apocalypse*. But there are other elements in it which, given the author and given the text he is explicating, might come as more of a surprise. Much of the book is wittily insouciant in tone; almost all of it shows a fertile, restless intelligence hard at work; in some respects it is a model of how to make a little learning go a long way. The resourcefulness with which Lawrence uses his reading of Nietzsche, of Burnet's *Early Greek Philosophy*, and of a few exegetical works on the book of Revelation, puts one in mind of T.S. Eliot's famous observation about how different our capacities are when it comes to drawing intellectual sustenance from the available sources: 'Some men can absorb knowledge, the more tardy must sweat for it. Shakespeare acquired more essential history from Plutarch than most could get from the whole British Museum.'

*

The Revelation of St John, also known simply as the Apocalypse, the last book of the Christian scriptures, is believed to have been written towards the end of the first century A.D. In form it is a Christian or Christianised version of a Jewish apocalypse. It has many of the characteristic features of the latter genre: visions of a final judgement and of cosmic warfare between the forces of good and evil; allegorical beasts and figures set against fantastic landscapes and heavenscapes; numerological clues to the date and order of the events described, which are connected in riddling fashion to actual personages and occurrences. All these elements are combined in a grandly obscure, divinely ordained settling of accounts for everyone and with everyone, sinners and saved alike.

As a mode of writing, apocalypse has often been described as the 'child' of classical Hebrew prophecy – and so it is: the bastard child, the child of woe and of hope endlessly deferred, and of dreams of a revenge become so grandiose that the earthly Jerusalem and circumjacent lands could no longer provide a stage big enough for its enactment. Classical Hebrew prophecy had itself been born out of despair and defeat, out of an attempt to understand how it could have happened that God's chosen people had been defeated by the Assyrians and Babylonians and driven out of the land that He had given them. In the apocalyptic writings which developed over a further several hundred years of defeat, chiefly at the hands of Seleucid Greeks and Romans, Yahweh's great scheme of redemption for Israel was enlarged beyond the bounds of this world and its kingdoms to take in the entire cosmos; it also became mixed up inextricably with astrology, angelology, demonology, and doctrines of the after-life and the last judgement – of which notions and preoccupations the classical prophetic texts had been innocent.

An 'enlargement' I have just called these writings; yet I find it impossible to read them without feeling that for the most part they are the product of smaller, crazier minds than those which had produced the most affecting of the prophetic books. In the apocalyptic writings, Yahweh's plan for Israel, which the prophets believed history would make splendidly manifest to all, has been reduced to a kind of secret code, shared between writer and reader; meaningless and often repulsive symbols whirl by phantasmagorically; paranoia and obsession reign virtually unchallenged, except by sudden lurches into bathos. ('When the Lamb opened the seventh seal, there was silence in heaven for about half an hour.')

Of all the apocalypses still extant, the Revelation to John is obviously the best known, by virtue of its inclusion in the biblical canon. Reading between the lines of some present-day Christian commentators one can sense a certain embarrassment at their having to 'own up', as it were, to the text. But they have little choice in the matter, ultimately, since apocalyptic elements abound in the Gospels and Epistles, and it is clear that the development of Christianity would have been inconceivable had such teachings and traditions not been widespread among the Jews of Palestine in Jesus's day. Other commentators, needless to say, are less inhibited: there are millions of believers all over the world to whom every reference and symbol in the Revelation, and all the dreamlike transformations they undergo, are fraught with a truth which is in their view far easier to discern than to live by.* And then there are all those people, readers of Lawrence and readers of nothing at all, who probably know little more of the book than a handful of phrases which have passed into the language: the Alpha and Omega;

---

* Some time ago a leaflet was pushed into my hand at a railway station. Quoting lavishly from the more lurid parts of the Revelation, it promised us (on earth) wars, earthquakes, and general destruction, and (in hell) eternal torments. These appalling prospects, it said, could be avoided by turning to Jesus and seeking from him the forgiveness which only he could give. BUT DON'T DELAY, the last line of the pamphlet proclaimed: THIS OFFER IS OPEN FOR A VERY LIMITED PERIOD ONLY.

Babylon, the great mother of harlots; the mark of the beast; the four horsemen; the seven seals; the blood of the lamb; a new heaven and a new earth; and so forth. At the very least they will recognise some of these phrases as the titles of motion pictures.

*

The Revelation, I said earlier, is the last book in the Christian Bible. There is a curiously touching symmetry to be found in the fact that *Apocalypse*, D.H. Lawrence's commentary on it, was the last book he wrote. There is also a curious appropriateness in Lawrence's turning to examine directly and explicitly the biblical apocalypse as the final act of his writing life, when he himself had spent so much time producing apocalypses of his own in novels, stories, essays, letters and poems. Though he did not know how ill he was at the time, he was a dying man when he was working on *Apocalypse*, and it was published only after his death.

In tone and style it resembles other works in that strange visionary-discursive genre which Lawrence invented as a vehicle for the development of his 'philosophy'. One of the striking things about this genre is that it often took the form of a literary criticism so wildly unconventional in character as to make Lawrence's 'ordinary' reviews and critical essays look positively meek. He would take a set of books which had affected him deeply, try to account for the effect they had had on him, and then go on to use the experience – the whole experience, an amalgam of the text and his response to it – as the basis for speculations and preachings of all kinds about life, history, art, society, education, politics, physiology, the ultimate nature of existence, and suchlike matters. *Study of Thomas Hardy* is such a book; so is *Studies in Classic American Literature*; so in effect are *Fantasia of the Unconscious* and *Psychoanalysis and the Unconscious*, for all Lawrence's denial in them of any radical indebtedness to the writings of Freud; so is *Apocalypse*, which was originally intended to be nothing more than an introduction to a book by a friend with a special interest in astrology and the occult.

It was not only in books such as these, of course, that Lawrence worked on his 'philosophy'. His earliest critics were given to complaining about the inclination of his novels to collapse either into an outright exposition of doctrine, or into a dramatised illustration of it; and the complaints have not let up since. What has been much less often noticed is that the avowedly philosophical or doctrinal books are always ready to undergo a somewhat similar process in reverse: they constantly threaten to turn into fiction (by which I mean more than that they state untruths), into poetry, or into autobiography. For instance, though *Apocalypse* ranges about in as uncontrolled and portentous a fashion as any book he ever wrote, its second chapter opens with a passage which plunges us at once into the world of his childhood and youth, and hence into that of the most touching and sardonic of his short stories:

102

And I remember, as a child, I used to wonder over the curious sense of self-glory which one felt in the uneducated leaders, the men especially of the Primitive Methodist Chapels. They were not on the whole pious or mealy-mouthed or objectionable, these colliers who spoke heavy dialect and ran the 'Pentecost'. They were certainly not humble or apologetic. No, they came in from the pit and sat down to their dinners with a bang, and their wives and daughters ran to wait on them, and their sons obeyed them without overmuch resentment . . . It was not until many years had gone by, and I had read something of comparative religion and the history of religion, that I realised what a strange book it was that had inspired the colliers on the black Tuesday nights in Pentecost or Beauvale Chapel to such a queer sense of authority and religious cheek. Strange marvellous black nights of the north Midlands, with the gas-light hissing in the chapel, and the roaring of the strong-voiced colliers. Popular religion: a religion of self-glorification and power, forever! and of darkness. No wailing 'Lead kindly Light' about it.

Does it matter, should it matter to us, that within a few pages of this genial recollection Lawrence is writing in quite another fashion about the spirit of 'self-glorification' which he believes to be directly inspired by the 'strange book' which is his subject?

. . . it is not the revenge one minds so much as the perpetual self-glorification of these saints and martyrs and their profound impudence. How one loathes them in their 'new white garments'. How disgusting their priggish rule must be! How vile is their spirit, really, insisting, simply insisting on wiping out the whole universe, bird and blossom, star and river, and above all, *everybody* except themselves and their precious 'saved' brothers. How beastly their new Jerusalem, where the flowers never fade, but stand in everlasting sameness! How terribly bourgeois, to have unfading flowers!

If you take *Apocalypse* to be nothing more than an interesting but incoherent rhapsody, then a discordance like the one just illustrated will seem not to matter at all. Those who believe Lawrence to have been incapable of serious thought will be confirmed in their view; just as those who prefer rhapsody to intellection (from Lawrence or anyone else) will be confirmed in theirs. Two things should stand in the way of either of these responses, however. The first is that for all its divagations, *Apocalypse*, like the other books in the Lawrencian genre to which it belongs, does have a fairly tight argumentative frame. The second is that the characteristic high spirits and fluency of the two passages quoted above – moving as easily as they do between a rage which is indistinguishable from relish, to a nostalgia indistinguishable from amusement – stand in an unexpected relationship to the apocalyptic strain in Lawrence's work as a whole. Or so I hope to show.

*

To deal with the argument of *Apocalypse* first. Like innumerable commentators before and since, Lawrence offers an interpretation of the Revelation, which he insists is the 'real' or most truthful one. Essentially he interprets the document as a palimpsest in which three main layers of meaning can be discerned. The first is a dream or drama of revenge, dictated by the underdog rancour of the sort of Judaism and Christianity of which it is representative. This part of the book owes a great deal to the Nietzsche of *The Anti-Christ*, though Lawrence can hardly be said to be generous in acknowledging his indebtedness. Like Nietzsche, Lawrence exalts 'heroic' or 'aristocratic' or 'personal' power, while speaking with little but contempt of what he sees as the disguised but implacable lust for power supposedly lurking within the Christian ideal of humility.

Then, within or beneath this layer, he discerns with rather more enthusiasm the remains of a Babylonian star-myth or astrological system. Hence the multitude of references to the heavenly bodies in the Revelation, like the one at the very beginning, to 'him who holds the seven stars in his right hand, who walks among the seven golden lampstands.' (This, according to Lawrence, is 'a Jesus very far from the [one] . . . in Gethsemane'; a Jesus 'who wheels the stars in the universal revolution of the heavens . . . a *Kosmokrator* and *Kosmodynamos*.') Within that again, he finds the nethermost layer of the Revelation to be a pagan 'mystery' or initiation rite of the kind associated with the Orphics and the votaries of Isis. This layer, Lawrence declares, has been either hidden by the later re-writers of the document, or moralised by them into the uniquely Christian version of the dying and reborn god. But the pagan gods, he insists, were many, and their rites and purposes knew nothing of 'boring', 'revenge-seeking', 'petty' morality; they knew nothing of 'the dead body and the postponed reward'; they were omnipresent gods of the moment, of forces, of things, who made manifest the 'potency' which belongs to mankind and to which mankind belongs.

So much for the scheme of interpretation. As for its ultimate polemical intention – well, he wishes to persuade us that we are at 'the very end of the Christian cycle . . . [and] *all* our present life-forms are evil.' Before us there is a choice between 'degeneration and decadence' on the one hand, or 'a deliberate return to the roots and a new start', on the other. We must not delude ourselves into believing that any other possibilities are open to us. And how would we know the 'new start', should we find it?

What man most wants is his living wholeness and living unison, not his own isolate salvation of his 'soul' . . . Whatever the dead and unborn may know, they cannot know the beauty, the marvel of being alive in the flesh. We ought to dance with rapture that we should be alive and in the flesh, and part of the living, incarnate cosmos . . . There is nothing of me that is alone and absolute except my mind, and we shall find that the mind has no existence by itself, it is only the glitter of the sun on the surface of the waters . . . I am a part of the great whole, and I can never escape. But I *can* deny my connections, break them, and become a fragment. Then I am wretched.

*

Utopian longings and prophetic rage; a conviction that he had been peculiarly chosen to instruct the bemired multitudes; an urgent belief that the entire, present order of things was doomed, that it deserved to be doomed, and that its end was coming on apace; a set of doctrines which he may have enunciated only spasmodically, and qualified ironically, but into which almost every historical and cultural phenomenon which came his way could be fitted – all these are aspects of Lawrence's fictions (from *The Rainbow* on) and teachings (from *Study of Thomas Hardy* on) which make Lawrence quite unmistakably an apocalyptic writer. Yet when it came to defining the state of affairs he longed for and looked to the future to bring, after the great collapse had taken place, Lawrence parted company sharply from all the other prophetic writers whom he might be thought to resemble, and after whom he would seem to have half-consciously modelled himself.

It was not that he tried to compete with other designers of perfect or heavenly worlds to come, and, like them, failed in making his particular version of it imaginatively plausible, let alone attractive. Nor was it that Lawrence, like the mystics, attempted to escape from this ever-recurring dilemma by in effect trying to abolish time and all forms of individuality in his visions. One might say that Lawrence's case was the very opposite of these. The 'new world' or the 'redeemed' condition he looked forward to, after the disintegration of the existing social and spiritual order, was always characterised by instability, openness, change, unpredictability; in a word (which he himself used on more than one occasion) *unfinishedness*. No marble halls here, let alone flowers that never fade; no immortal, disembodied spirits either. On the contrary. The supreme value he put on flux and inconclusiveness was absolutely indistinguishable from his belief that there could be no redemption outside the flesh. Indeed, the notion of a spiritual life that was not also incarnate repelled him, in so far as he found it at all imaginable. Because he wanted us to see life, collectively and individually, and consciousness, and even natural form, as so many ever-provisional forays into the unknown and the indefinable, he claimed that what he hated most about the modern world was its mental-spiritual fixity of purpose, its determination to know *a priori* what is right or good or at least profitable and to proceed accordingly. In other words, as he puts it in *Apocalypse*, he could not tolerate the 'illusion' of Christian and materialist alike that 'there is somewhere to go to'.

For an apocalyptic writer – who might be defined most simply as one who prophesies grand finales – to recoil from the idea of 'somewhere to go to' (while telling us exactly where we are going) is paradoxical enough. We have already seen that in *Women in Love* Lawrence willed us, with all his might, not-to-will. In *A Propos of Lady Chatterley* he instructs us, through the abstract medium of the printed word, to avoid having sex in the head. The paradox we are looking at here has something in common with these. But it leads to a more striking paradox still. For if the highest value is to be put on indeterminacy, on what is open and unfinished, on what is forever tremblingly in the balance, then we are entitled to ask where in Lawrence's own work those values are most clearly manifested; where we are shown most fiercely and most tenderly what it feels like to live in the condition of uncertainty and of emotional intensity they suggest. And if we ask this question, the answer that comes at once is that never were his people to be so open to themselves, to one another, and to everything around them, so uncertain of what lay ahead and yet so eager to reach it, as they were in *Sons and Lovers* and in the dozens of stories he wrote about the mining Midlands of his childhood and youth. Indeed, a reader of *Apocalypse* cannot but see something of the sense of wonder I am speaking of, and the wit that so often accompanies it, flare up again in the description quoted earlier of those Primitive Methodist preachers of his boyhood.

If this is the case, then what follows from it is both important and unexpected. It means that the 'new worlds' and the 'new life' sought for by this apocalyptic writer, this sweeper away of our present corruptions, were actually to be found somewhere behind him, in the world he had abandoned, amid the despoiled landscapes he had come to regard with such horror by the end of his life.

It is not only there that they are to be found, of course; but chiefly there. It was Lawrence himself who told us, 'Never trust the teller; trust the tale.' In thinking of him as an apocalyptic writer we could do worse than follow his advice.

FOURTEEN

UP AT THE RANCH

◆

One of the functions that took place during the D.H. Lawrence Festival in Santa Fe, which was held to celebrate the fiftieth anniversary of his death, was a procession to the shrine on the Lawrence ranch, outside Taos. A few hundred people must have taken part in the ceremony. After listening to a string quartet play Schubert (and after a tense, scrambling, ill-organised journey in a fleet of buses and cars from Santa Fe), the participants formed up in a line. A drum was beaten somewhere in front, girls in white robes went ahead scattering flowers, and the procession zig-zagged up the path from the ranch house to the little concrete structure in which Lawrence's ashes are reputedly incorporated. In front of it is the tombstone of Frieda Lawrence, and of her third husband, Angelo Ravagli; in the gable above is the phoenix symbol, in stone or cement, which Lawrence had adopted as his own.

There, while the clouds spattered down some drops of rain, and the wind hissed among the swaying pines, an actor and an actress read extracts from Lawrence's writings on New Mexico. The actor was dressed in a khaki jacket and trousers of a somewhat military cut; the actress was preternaturally red in the cheeks and black about the eyes. Somebody else played a flute solo. Then people filed into the little hut to sign the visitor's book. Subsequently, back on the campus of the College of Santa Fe, where a conference on Lawrence's work was taking place, an American professor notorious for the forthrightness of his speech described the process as 'obscene'. To me it had seemed just absurd and vaguely humiliating. It reminded me a little of all those other, *ad hoc* ceremonial occasions trying to make a stab at solemnity which one sees from time to time on television: the crowning of the Sportswoman of the Year, say, or perhaps the accession to independence and full nationhood of some tiny island in the middle of the Pacific.

About ten days later, in a place called Questa just south of the Colorado border, I saw a procession of a different kind. Questa was a bare, sprawling scatter of clapboard habitations and stores in the foothills of the Rockies, with bristling mountains on one side of the highway, and nothing very much on the other. The place appeared to be full of failures: dilapidated hoardings, boarded-up windows, broken roofs. Hank's Auto Spares had obviously done no business for a year or two; the same seemed to be true of the Emmanuel Deliverance Church; the same of Betty's Beauty Salon, a tin box with shuttered windows and an open door hanging askew. It was a hot, dry, windless day; the pines on the mountains had monopolised all the available shade, leaving none for Questa and the exposed flank of semi-desert on the other side. On the high road, about thirty young men and women, dressed in rags, sandals, thongs, gauze, copper bangles, feathers, ribbons, tank-tops, and other such finery, formed themselves up into processional order. A girl carrying a red and black flag marched at the head of them, and a saffron-robed, shaven-headed Oriental brought up the rear. Two or three were carrying pikes decorated with streamers on which mystic symbols were inscribed; another couple were carrying shallow drums, rather like tambourines without bells. There were whites among them, blacks, several Orientals, people who could have been Mexicans.

At a signal from the girl with the flag they struck their drums, a small chant rose to the sky, and they began marching alongside the highway. They were as ragged, as devout and self-involved, as some medieval band on an old woodcut. One might have imagined them marching from village to village, between heathlands or cultivated fields, with one pointed church-steeple signalling the way to the next, above the horizon. But amid those stunning, excessive distances, on that bald highway, against the side of that mountain, they appeared to be of no more consequence than so many ants toiling along the bank of a ditch. From where had they come? Where were they going? The nearest place, east or west, was thirty miles distant. There was no vehicle in sight that could have brought them to Questa, or that was going to take them away. On they marched. Tap, tap, tap, went their little drums. Trample, shuffle, trample, went their bare or sandalled feet on the side of the road.

They infuriated the driver of the car ahead of mine at the filling-station. He was a plump, busy, heavily belted man, dressed in the inevitable pair of jeans and a braggartly off-white Stetson hat. His car had a Texan numberplate; his wife, mother, and children sat inside it. 'We don't want any more of that sort . . . We got enough of 'em already, you bet . . . There go your tax-dollars, feeding and keeping 'em . . . You see that one with the flag to stop the traffic? She wouldn't stop us in Texas . . . Yeah, one sideswipe and there'd be twenty of 'em gone . . .' These remarks were directed at the wizened proprietor of the place, who wore a long-peaked cap with the name of a brand of oil stitched on it, and who agreed, though without much vehemence, to everything his customer said. It was extraordinary how threatened the Texan appeared to feel by that procession on the road below; but one just had to look at the flushed face under the brim of his hat to see also that it was precisely the vulnerability and forlornness of the pilgrims that had excited his malevolence. Yet for all his words, he did nothing.

By the time my car had been filled with petrol he was gone. The pilgrims had perhaps covered two hundred yards on their march to nowhere.

*

I wonder what that Texan would have said if he had known that valuable tax-dollars had been expended to bring me to New Mexico, too, along with a group of other British writers and various Beat American poets and novelists (California vintage '57), and academics from different universities, to consider such issues as 'D.H. Lawrence and Modernism' and 'The Influence of D.H. Lawrence on the Naturalistic Novel'. Participating in our cogitations was an audience of several hundred who had paid handsomely for the privilege of attending (and had thus presumably relieved some of the strain on the pocket-book of the Texan.) Almost all these participants were white, middle-class, and middle-aged, though there were some students among them. Many of those I spoke to, both among the young and the middle-aged, wanted to be writers, and seemed to think that attending conferences of this kind would somehow help them to fulfil their ambitions. A few, very few, were intensely knowledgeable and passionate Lawrencians.

There were morning sessions, afternoon sessions, and lengthy breaks for refreshment. Occasionally the proceedings were interrupted by moments of the kind of unintentional comedy that always arises at such gatherings. When William Burroughs, author of *Naked Lunch* – wearing a grey suit, a grey tie, and the look of the pastor of a backstreet spiritualist chapel who has no misgivings about the world to come, but a few about making ends meet in this one – was asked about D.H. Lawrence's influence on subsequent fiction, he replied that *he* had been influenced by *The Plumed Serpent*. That, he seemed to feel, exhausted the possibilities of the entire subject. When an English critic and D.H. Lawrence biographer declared that every great writer needed 'courage, discipline, and intelligence', I happened to see the girl in front of me, with an open notebook on her lap, solemnly copy down these desiderata in a column, which she then carefully boxed in. What, I wondered, would she do with the list when she got home? Learn it off by heart? Give marks to all the writers she subsequently read on the Courage-Discipline-Intelligence Scale? Be unable to remember the occasion when the words were uttered and to whom exactly they were supposed to apply? A great soldier, maybe? A great explorer? A secondary schoolteacher? In the meantime, this critic, speaking manfully of 'integrity', 'independence', 'wholeness' and so forth, as though saying the words was the same thing as displaying the qualities, had gone on to urge us to buy his book on Ted Hughes, for six dollars and ninety-five cents, which he described as 'far more important' than his book on Lawrence.

Wallowing about over many square miles of dusty desert, Santa Fe has no public transport of any kind, not even any taxis; the participants in the conference were thus wholly dependent upon the transport arrangements made by the organisers. This led to many tense, not to say paranoiac, moments; but on the whole the arrangements worked better than might have been expected. Some cars were driven by handsome young men in blazers who worked for the college; most were in the hands of local girls who had been specially enrolled for the occasion. These girls wanted (variously) to write; to paint; to illustrate children's books; to 'work in leather and fabrics'; to do silver-smithing; to study a subject, Suggestology, of which I had never heard before, and which had something to do with hemispheric dominance in the brain; one wanted to build kites for a living, but first intended spending some time in Colorado, on her own, in a tent, while she 'got her head together'. Santa Fe (like Taos, on a smaller scale) catered lavishly for all such activities. Whole streets were given over to art galleries. The summer homes of millionaires occupied all the finest buttresses and coigns of vantage. A notice-board in a local launderette was covered with advertisements for 'Holistic Fitness in Personal Health'; 'The HQ for Spiritual, Metaphysical and Self-Development'; 'Guatemalan Clothes, Bags, Weaving'; 'Genji Karate'; 'How You Can Get in Touch with You'; and 'The Healing Arts (Massage, Macrobiotics) and Various Expressive Forms (Drawing, Dance, Bongos)'.

The mountains looked down on all of this, and more; and from our motel rooms, while we waited for transport, we looked up at the mountains through a mesh of electricity and telephone wires, hanging just above a jagged frieze of neon signs, of giant trucks parked in herds on stretches of asphalt, and of the random roof-lines of the Sizzlin' Steak House, the Biggest Car Muffler Dealer in New Mexico, the Santa Fe Roller Disco, and the rest. Beyond all these was the desert. Flat, pallid surfaces almost entirely devoid of growth alternated with fishback rises, dotted with juniper trees about the height of a man. The higher the rises, the taller were the trees upon them. From some points on the outskirts of the city nothing could be seen but such plains and spotted slopes, in alternate stripes or corrugations, going back a hundred miles to the horizon; elsewhere, at lesser distances, the mountains rose up at angles to one another and to the sky. The colours of the desert were yellow, biscuit, ash, rose, brick, silvery green, sullen green. Hardly a human mark or scratch was to be seen beyond the mess of the city; but if you went out along the highways you would find at intervals, under bloated plastic and neon signs, all-American strips or zips of hamburger joints, motels, gas-stations, and used-car lots. Then desert and mountains again, until the next desolate, garish strip – desolate both because of the overpowering emptiness of the spaces around them, and because of the notion of what is human, alive, companionable, entertaining, *necessary*, that these places reveal. The emptier the country, the more intensely did the people who live in each rickety, haphazard cluster of buildings apparently feel the need to assert themselves; the more strident their self-assertion, the more intolerable still the silence beyond them.

The landscapes of New Mexico and Colorado are the most dramatic I have ever seen: not even those of Southern Africa are more stark and imposing; or bring together such heights with such widths, such bareness with so much swarthy growth; or have unleashed above them such spectacular electric storms, with cat-like leapings of lightning from the mountain-tops into the valleys. It is a curious fact that, with a few exceptions, like Mark Twain or the historian Francis Parkman, American writers have on the whole failed to make imaginatively available to their readers the splendour of the country's landscapes. More often they merely offer, in Whitmanesque fashion, catalogues of what the country contains. Being there, one can more readily understand their failure. Again and again one finds oneself flinching away from the view, almost as if one were dazzled by a very bright light: it is too much, incommensurate with everything else, one's own consciousness not least. The movie-makers have done better than the writers in conveying the sense both of oppression and of release that this can produce.

As for Lawrence, nothing he ever saw or felt was beyond the reach of his pen. No one to my knowledge has written better than him about New Mexico; this in itself was some kind of justification for the attempt that was being made by the locals to 'kidnap' him. ('I suppose that if this conference were being held in Australia,' an English writer said tartly at one point, 'it would be all about *Kangaroo.*') I could remember being much moved by my first reading, many years ago, of the lyrical description of the ranch which brings *St Mawr* to an end; but it was not until I visited the place, and then spent a few days in Taos, that I realised how much of the power of the passage springs from its literal accuracy – whether it be in speaking of the dust-storms that sweep across the plain, or of the 'blackish crack' of the Rio Grande Valley, or of the curved 'outwatching' mountains above. But that is not all. What fills out the description, what makes us feel as we read it that the landscape is yielding its secrets to the language, even while the language itself is being shaped by the landscape, is that it is also a passionately sympathetic and amused history of the ranch, and of all the human efforts at taming the wilderness which had finally petered out at that very spot. Written, what is more, when conditions up there must have been incomparably more arduous than they are now, by a man who knew his own state of health to be constantly at the very edge of a total collapse.

*

Lawrence had a taste (at least on paper) for home-made cults, processions, and ceremonials; in novels like *The Plumed Serpent* and tales like 'The Woman Who Rode Away' he indulged it to excess. He also had strongly developed messianic impulses; the lonelier he felt himself to be, and the more his work was vilified and persecuted, the stronger those impulses became. All that said, one can still be pretty sure that he would have loathed the reverential procession to the shrine on the ranch, as well as the conference; not to speak of the other concurrent, festive events: a fancy-dress ball at Taos, an open-air recital of his works in Santa Fe. Those obscure pilgrims in Questa would probably have roused his sympathy and curiosity more than all the literary folk who came to the shrine. Yet I suspect that he would have despised the pilgrims for looking so messy and pathetic; being the kind of person he was, he would probably also have chosen to take exception to the mixture of races among them.

Of course, everyone who took part in the festival was at least intermittently conscious of the ironies of the whole affair. Lawrence despised tourism; yet here he was being used as a tourist attraction. He hated the enlightened, well-to-do middle-class; yet here, at the open-air recital, were his most bitingly satirical and contemptuous poems about the bourgeoisie being read by stars like Elizabeth Taylor and Eve-Marie Saint, to whoops of delight from a well-to-do, enlightened, middle-class audience. He was (to put it moderately) unenthusiastic about academics; yet here were numbers of professors competing for what one can only call 'bits' of Lawrence, and comparing this conference with the one held last year in North Carolina or South Dakota. Lawrence spent much of his working life wondering how he would pay the rent for one tumbledown cottage after another; yet here were thousands of dollars, from private, state, and federal funds being spent to create around him and his work a grand occasion for Santa Fe. One further ironic circumstance, which I admit occurred to me only after the conference was over, was that almost all the writers and professors who took part in it were older than Lawrence was at the time of his death.

Underneath all this however, there is a yet deeper irony. The fact is that if you are a great writer, which Lawrence was, and if in addition you set yourself up as a prophet and guide to all mankind, which Lawrence did, this is the kind of thing that is bound to happen to you – eventually. In the long run, the wishes of the public are always much, much stronger than those of the people to whom it chooses to do reverence.

PART FIVE

SOUTH AFRICAN

FIFTEEN

OLIVE SCHREINER

A colonial culture is one which has no memory. The discontinuities of colonial experience make it almost inevitable that this should be so. A political entity brought into existence by the actions of an external power; a population consisting of the descendants of conquerors, of slaves and indentured labourers, and of dispossessed aboriginals; a language in the courts and schools which has been imported like an item of heavy machinery; a prolonged economic and psychological subservience to a metropolitan centre a great distance away . . . One hardly needs to labour the point that such conditions make it extremely difficult for any section of the population to develop a vital, effective belief in the past as a present concern, and in the present as a consequence of the past's concerns.

The passage of time alone cannot cure the condition; nor a self-assertive nationalism; nor for that matter political independence. However, it must not be supposed that the absence of a memory, in the terms defined above, need inhibit the perpetuation of fierce historical enmities. On the contrary. Because the sense of history is so deficient, these enmities tend to be regarded as so many given, unalterable facts of life, phenomena of nature, as little open to human change or question as the growth of leaves in spring or the movement of clouds across the sky. Until very recently a white South African, for example, felt no need to ask himself how the black man came to be his inferior; he simply knew that the black man *was* inferior.

So it is perfectly possible to live without a memory; in some ways it can be positively more comfortable to do so. In any case, one does not miss what one has never had. 'Fancy,' Olive Schreiner wrote of her fellow white South Africans in 1890, after her first prolonged spell of residence in Europe, 'fancy a whole nation of lower-middle-class philistines, without an aristocracy of blood or intellect or muscular labourers to save them.' A century later her words still convey with painful accuracy a certain truth about the structure of white South African society as a whole, and especially about the English-speaking group to which she herself belonged.

In her time the South African English were the dominant group in local politics. Since then they have seen that responsibility taken from them by their former great rivals for political supremacy, the Afrikaners (or Boers). Now the English-speakers turn this way and that, radically divided among themselves, as the Afrikaners and the black majority of the population meet in a fierce struggle for power: a struggle which in effect began with the Dutch settlement of the Cape more than three hundred years ago, and which may still, in circumstances utterly different from any we can imagine today, be alive three hundred years hence. (Look at Ireland, after all; and there are other parts of the world which come to mind by way of analogy.) Over the last century English-speaking South Africans have made an indispensable contribution at every level to the transformation of the country from the backward, empty colony it once was to the powerful yet somehow prospectless industrial state it has become. They themselves have grown wealthy; the institutions they have established, and their connections with the outside world, have helped to form the cultural and political consciousness even of those groups, like the Afrikaners, with whom they have been most in rivalry. But time and money notwithstanding, they have managed to remain a nation of lower-middle-class philistines. Blankness rules; blankness perpetuates itself.

*

In an essay on Edgar Allan Poe, an American poet of a later generation, Allen Tate, has written of how difficult it was for him as a fellow Southerner, indeed as a fellow Virginian, to 'evaluate' Poe. 'He is with us', Tate wrote,

> like a dejected cousin: we may 'place' him, but we cannot exclude him from our board. This is the recognition of a relationship, almost of the blood, which we must in honour acknowledge: what destroyed him is potentially destructive of us. Not only this; we must acknowledge another obligation ... the obligation of loyalty to one's experience: he was in our lives and we cannot pretend that he was not.

The difficulty I have in trying to evaluate the work of Olive Schreiner is of a precisely similar kind. She was in my experience and I cannot pretend otherwise. Indeed, the first literary pilgrimage I ever made, though I was hardly of an age to think of it as such, was to her grave, near the village of Cradock in the Cape Province. I must have been about eight or nine years old at the time. I can remember my father stopping the car (we were going on a family holiday to Port Elizabeth) on one of those dusty, interminable roads that led from one miserable, tin-roofed Karroo dorp to the next, with distances of fifty miles and more between each cluster of habitations. We climbed through a wire fence and made our way up the steep sides of a kopje, littered like every other with enormous black boulders and dotted here and there with nondescript shrubs and bushes. On

116

the summit of the kopje was the igloo-shaped stone cairn in which are buried Olive Schreiner, her husband, her infant daughter, and her favourite dog. The view beneath was of a red and brown expanse stretching flat to the horizon on all sides, interrupted only by stony kopjes like the one on which we were standing, and by the glint of water from a half-empty dam. It was shaped like a thumbnail and looked no bigger than a thumbnail, too, from the height we were at. I can remember how impressed I was by the sun-scorched aridity and solitude of the scene; and also how obscurely creditable or virtuous I felt our own presence there to be.

My parents had stopped the car because Olive Schreiner was a part of their experience too. My mother had always admired *The Story of an African Farm*, and it was at her urging that I was to read it for the first time shortly after our visit to the grave. But if she admired Olive Schreiner as a novelist, she admired her still more as a feminist. As for my father, the first public meeting he had ever attended in his life had been one held in the Cape Town City Hall, organised to protest against the Kishinev Pogroms in Russia, in 1905. At the meeting a special message from Olive Schreiner, entitled 'A Letter on the Jew', had been read out by her husband to great applause. My father never forgot her message of solidarity, and how directly he had felt it speak to his own condition, as an immigrant youth who was taking his first tentative step into South African life at that very gathering.

Yet it remains indicative of the almost incredible 'blankness' I spoke of earlier that not until I was an adult did I learn that Olive Schreiner, the first and for many years the only South African writer to win a substantial reputation and readership outside her own country, had actually spent several years of her life, as a girl and as a middle-aged woman, in Kimberley, my own home-town. No one had thought the fact worth mentioning: no schoolmaster teaching English literature; no civic dignitary making a speech extolling the virtues of his city; no reporter on the local daily looking around for a little local colour. And this in spite of the fact that the house she lived in is still standing: or so I believe, after looking at contemporary maps of the town, in which 'Miss Schreiner's House' is quite specifically indicated, and then visiting the site.

There is nothing at all imposing about the house. It is a claustrophobically low, small cottage of corrugated iron, like all others of that period of the town's history, with a small wooden stoep in front of it and an exceptionally thick hedge of cypress bushes on three sides of it. The hedge makes it seem so much the more constricted and airless within. To call the area around the house a 'suburb' is to dignify it unnecessarily. It can have changed little since she lived there, though when I last visited it the inhabitants were Cape Coloureds, not whites. Unlit, unpaved, undemarcated, it consists merely of a random scatter of houses even meaner than Olive Schreiner's, with winding tracks through the sand connecting one house with another. There are some thorn-trees; a few ragged sloots to carry rainwater away; the tailings of an abandoned mine on one side, and on the other the road to Barkly West, the site of the very first diamond-rush in the country. Kimberley itself, with its iron roofs and mine-dumps, is a couple of miles away: hardly more than a series of dark protuberances from the flat, unkempt, irredeemable waste spaces around it.

*

Still, however makeshift her surroundings in Kimberley may have been, however bleak and insignificant the dorps like Cradock and De Aar in which she lived for long periods, one wonders if they were really any less desolate than the London boarding-houses and hired lodgings which, early and late in her life, were the only other homes she knew. One wonders whether the company of pastoral Boers and philistine English South Africans could possibly have been more crippling to her talent than that, say, of the Fellowship of the New Life in London (whose prime, stated 'Object' as a Fellowship was 'The cultivation of a perfect character in each and all').

Havelock Ellis, the prophetically bewhiskered author of all those studies in the psychology of a sexual act which he himself was incapable of performing; Edward Carpenter, the gentle homosexual author of tracts on the rights both of women and what he referred to as 'the intermediate sex'; Eleanor, Karl Marx's gifted and tragic daughter, who was finally driven to suicide by her lover, Edward Aveling, the notorious socialist, swindler, and ladies' man ... about such late-Victorian secularists, advanced thinkers, progressives, feminists, translators of Ibsen, indefatigable founders of societies and discussion groups, it is easier, I admit, to be ironic than to be just. That they failed so often to live up to their ideals would in itself be little enough to hold against them. We all fail at that task. But that they should have abstained from drawing conclusions about the nature of their ideals, the ambitions they nourished for all mankind, from the manifold miseries and complexities of their own lives, let alone the lives of others – that is another matter, and one which any reader who has exposed himself to the collected writings of Olive Schreiner is likely to find harder to forgive.

One sees plainly enough why she was drawn to their company. She had arrived in England in 1881 – 'England at last!' she wrote in her diary – bringing with her the manuscript of *The Story of an African Farm*, as well as drafts of two other novels, neither of which was to be published until after her death. She was then twenty-six years old: a missionary's daughter whose rejection of her parents' beliefs had been all the more painful and guilt-laden, not less so, for having taken place at a very early age. (She stated that she had irrevocably ceased to believe in God at the age of ten, after the death of a much-loved younger sister; the evidence of her books suggests that practically from babyhood she had loathed the Calvinistic doctrines which her father was trying to spread among the tribesmen on the frontiers of the colony.) She was an intellectual who had never gone to a school of even the most rudimentary kind, and who throughout her adolescence and early womanhood had met practically no one with whom she could discuss the books that came into her hands. She was a hater of injustice and cruelty, whose imagination was inclined to dwell obsessively on images of torture and blood-letting. She was a feminist who – almost inevitably, one feels – appears to have been seduced and jilted at the age of sixteen. She was talented, lonely, neurotic, and afflicted with a variety of psychosomatic ailments; capable of suffering deeply, and yet with a most uncertain grasp on her own experience; energetic and ambitious, but always prone to flee from the circumstances of her life into an uplifting and uplifted rhetoric which was not merely 'abstract', but all too personal, patently self-justifying and self-condoling, as well.

Behind her was an unhappy childhood, spent on isolated mission stations; an early departure, at the age of twelve, from her parents' home; some years spent in keeping house for her older brothers and sisters; more years spent as a governess for various families of Boer farmers, mostly in the district of Cradock; much reading of the works of writers like Mill, Emerson, Darwin and Herbert Spencer. (The incident of Waldo's encounter with the stranger in *The Story of an African Farm* is based upon a chance meeting she had had with a travelling government official, who was so impressed by her intellectual ardour, and so amazed at meeting such a girl on a mission station in one of the remotest corners of the colony, that he passed on to her his copy of Herbert Spencer's *First Principles*. Pretty dry fare, we might today feel, for an imaginative girl; but she did not find it so. 'I always think that when Christianity burst upon the dark Roman world it was what that book was to me,' she wrote years later.) Throughout this period she had been under attack from members of her family and her friends for her 'freethinking'; throughout she had been writing her fictions, and dreaming of an escape to a larger, freer society than any she had yet seen, to a deeper and more comprehending love than any she had yet known.

The Story of an African Farm was accepted by Chapman & Hall about a year after her arrival in England. The sole editorial suggestion they made was that Lyndall, the heroine of the book, should marry the man whose child she bears – otherwise they said, 'Smith's, the railway booksellers, would not put it on their stalls'. Olive Schreiner of course declined to make any such change. Published at first under the pseudonym of 'Ralph Iron', the book was an immediate success with reviewers and the reading public. Eminent political and literary figures of the day, ranging from Gladstone to Shaw and Oscar Wilde, spoke well of the book, met its author, and spoke well of her too. 'Jewish-looking' was a phrase some of her new acquaintances used, admiringly it would seem, to describe her appearance: she was stockily built, but vital in her movements; her dark hair was exceptionally thick; her brown eyes exceptionally bright. Havelock Ellis, who was then a beginner in the world of letters, wrote a favourable review of the book; he and she started a correspondence, which led to their meeting; soon she began to fall in love with him, and he with her. 'I think of you', she wrote to him, 'like a tall angel, as you looked at the Progressive meeting.'

A success story? A provincial girl emerging triumphantly into the great world?

So it would seem: even if her affair with Ellis was bound to lead to disappointment to them both. (They remained close friends, nevertheless, until the end of her life.) In fact, her letters over the next five or six years are – with some remissions, some periods of relative calm – a catalogue of physical and mental affliction; so much so that at times one begins to doubt her sanity, though not the extent of her sufferings. If her husband and biographer was eventually to say of her first year in London, when she had been unknown, that 'she spent much of her time crying . . . and was taking bromide of potassium more or less continuously in large doses', she herself recorded enough of the miseries she underwent when she was, as she put it, 'a fine genius, a celebrity [whom] tomorrow all these people would tread under their feet.' In her letters she writes of fever, burning, asthma, bleeding to death, her veins on fire, delirium, swellings, suffocations, madness and anguish, a terrible headache that never goes, vomiting, agony in the stomach, periodic pains, biting at her hands and knocking her head, years of darkness and weakness . . . and she diagnoses her own complaints with a cry that rings out unforgettably from the pages of her *Collected Letters*: 'Oh it isn't my chest, it isn't my legs, it's me, myself. What shall I do? Where shall I go?'

*

What she did, after eight years of wandering about England and the continent, was to return to South Africa. In many ways her decision was a wise one. Almost immediately her letters become calmer and happier in tone. One sees at once just how much of a strain her rootlessness and expatriation had been; her sense of belonging nowhere and – in spite of the confused intensity of her relationships with various men and women at different times – to no one. She was received with much honour in the colony; she knew herself to be one of its leading personalities; her position was all the stronger because in her absence her younger brother had successfully established himself in local politics, and was to become Prime Minister of the Cape Colony before the end of the decade. Within a few years of her return she met a young, handsome farmer-politician of English stock, and married him. Out of deference to her feminist sentiments, her husband added her name to his. Though the marriage was hardly an easy one for either of them, and though she and her husband were to spend very little time together in later years (without ever formally separating), it is clear that she got more personal happiness and fulfilment out of the marriage than out of any other relationship of her life.

Moreover, she had returned at a time when South African affairs were entering a particularly dramatic period. Cecil John Rhodes, who had become prime minister of the Cape in 1890, and who dreamed of seeing the Union Jack fly over Africa from the Cape to Cairo, had recently succeeded in having annexed into the British Empire the territory that was to be called Rhodesia for six or seven decades, and is now Zimbabwe; he was also busy fomenting the series of crises that led to the outbreak of war between Great Britain and the Boer Republics of the Transvaal and the Orange Free State in 1899. After a brief period of flirtation with the inveterately woman-hating Rhodes – and the word 'flirtation' should be used to describe more than her political attitudes towards him – she turned decisively against him and his policies, and began to use her pen in a series of polemical articles that roused much attention both in South Africa and Great Britain. Her comments on South Africa's political and social problems have on the whole proved far more perceptive and durable than those of the 'realists' of the time. She did not believe that the Boers would be or could be crushed by war; she opposed the insatiable annexationist ambitions of Rhodes in the far north, and exposed the cruelty with which some of his henchmen carried them out; she defended the rights of the blacks in all the territories involved in the struggle between Boer and Briton.* None of these were easy or popular attitudes to adopt, least of all during the Anglo-Boer War itself, when because of her 'pro-Boer' attitudes she was considered a potential traitor by the British and for a time was kept under conditions hardly better than those of house-arrest. Her courage and steadfastness (and her husband's, it should be added) were exemplary.

But again, there is another side to the picture. In one of the letters she wrote two or three years after first arriving in England, she had said, 'If I leave England, though I live for fifty years, still I am dead. The one fixed, unchanging dream of my life was to come; to have to go back makes life all a blank, nothing left.' Clearly she was wrong in every respect – in every respect, perhaps, but one. That is, her return to South Africa may well have been the end of her as a novelist. It is impossible, of course, to say that had she remained in Europe she would have finished *From Man to Man*, the novel she had started after *The Story of an African Farm*; or that she would have had the critical objectivity to extricate from what she had written of it those chapters which contain the best writing she ever did – the firmest, the most penetrating, the most original technically, surpassing easily even the best sections of *The Story of an African Farm*. (The other, quite separable chapters of the unfinished novel simply go on and on in her most intolerably uplifting and self-indulgent strain.) It may be that the book would have remained chaotically disorganised and unfinished whatever she did, wherever she lived. What is certain, however, is that the references to the novel in her letters show that all the work that was effectively to be done upon it had been completed before her return to South Africa. As she brought it back, so it was left at her death thirty years later, though throughout those decades she continued to speak

---

* It is striking, though, that despite her anti-imperialist attitudes, it never occurred to her to question the right of the white man to come into Southern Africa, provided he did so as a genuine settler and not just as a freebooter. Today the undesirability or even the immorality of colonisation of that kind would be regarded as axiomatic by practically everybody of liberal or radical views. Some may take this as evidence of a great advance in our social conscience over the last hundred years; others as proof of just how difficult it is at all times – ours as much as hers – to think outside the limits prescribed by an obscure *Zeitgeist*.

in patently self-deluding fashion of finishing it – one day.*

It is impossible to read *From Man to Man* without feeling an almost overwhelming sense of talents wasted and frustrated in a way that appears to have been both helpless and deliberate. From such a spectacle, from the wreckage of this potentially first-class work, one cannot turn with any sense of real satisfaction to her political writings on South Africa, compelling though her insights and sentiments are. Much the same is true of *Woman and Labour*, her one extended attempt at dealing with 'The Woman Question', which caused some stir in Europe and the United States on its publication in 1911. A dissatisfaction with *Woman and Labour*, at any rate, need not spring from any inclination automatically to put a higher value on 'art' than on a preoccupation with social or political issues; or from the feeling that relations between the sexes have so changed that everything she had to say has simply gone out of date. In fact, like her writings on South African politics, *Woman and Labour* is of value both as a document from the past and for insights which some readers will still feel to be relevant today. However, even the most perfervid Women's Liberationist is unlikely to see it as 'the bible of the women's movement', as some of its more enthusiastic admirers declared it to be at the time.†

The reason for the relative failure of the book is not far to seek. I have already suggested that theoretical or polemical writings of any kind presented peculiar temptations to Olive Schreiner, and in *Woman and Labour* she fell into them with the greatest readiness and regularity. Paradoxical though it may seem, for her to write on such topical issues of the day as the condition of women, or the relationship which should exist between white and black, or between Briton and Boer, was all too often not an act of engagement with the world immediately around her, but a sanctioned escape from it. She invariably took upon herself the pain of speaking up for the humiliated and oppressed – Boers, blacks, women, Jews; and what could be more selfless than that? She always pleaded for tenderness and candour in human relationships; and what could be more generous? She always tried to envisage a future in which mankind's finest aspirations would be realized; and what could be more hopeful and undaunted?

---

* *Trooper Peter Halkett of Mashonaland* (1897) is not really a novel. It is merely a brief, allegorised polemic against Rhodes, his British South Africa Charter Company, and the bloody repression of the Mashona 'rebellion' which had broken out in Rhodesia.

† Though there is no reason to suppose that she had ever read Karl Marx's work – in spite of her friendship with Eleanor and her flattering references to Marx in her 'Letter on the Jew' – some of her comments in the book do have an almost Marxist ring. For example: 'The women of no race or class will ever rise in revolt or attempt to bring about a revolutionary adjustment of their relationship to society, however intense their suffering and however clear their perception of it, while the welfare and persistence of their society requires their submission . . . Wherever there is a general attempt on the part of the women of any society to readjust their position in it, a close analysis will always show that the changed or changing conditions of that society have made women's acquiescence no longer necessary or desirable.' Or, as she puts it more succinctly elsewhere in the book: 'Other machinery; other duties.'

But again and again the effect of these espousals would be to transcend the torments of the present by a feat of moral and rhetorical levitation which ultimately strikes the reader as having an inner meaning or impulsion quite opposite to that intended. It begins to strike him as strangely selfish, uncaring, preoccupied more with reassuring the speaker – especially with the picture it presents to her of her own moral nobility – than with ministering to the needs of those to whom, or of whom, she is speaking. She is far from the only writer loudly asserting a love of humanity in whose work such a process can be observed.

The relevance of this mode of lacerated self-exaltation to several passages of *The Story of an African Farm* should be plain to any reader of the novel. Take, for example, the fable of The Hunter, which the stranger tells to Waldo in a central scene of the novel. (It was subsequently reprinted separately in a volume entitled *Dreams*, of which Olive Schreiner was particularly proud.) The fable describes how a Hunter leaves the comfortable valleys where the mass of mankind lives, and begins to scale an impassable mountain in search of the great white bird of truth he believes he will find on its summit. His utter loneliness and suffering are described at some length, and so too is the recompense he at last receives, when a single feather from the wing of the bird flutters down to him as he is on the point of dying. But within this allegory, one cannot help noticing, is buried another allegory of whose meaning the author was quite unconscious. The truth whose value and beauty we are so pressingly asked to believe in has, by definition, no connection whatsoever with any life that is actually lived down in the valley; and the same goes for the Hunter's manner of pursuing it. His truth hasn't even the merit of being death itself. No wonder he never asks himself what he could possibly do with the bird if he were ever to get his hands on it.

No, a much more modest truth we can catch on the wing is that it is only as a novelist, and only so far as she was one, that Olive Schreiner ever managed to engage herself wholly with the realities of the world as she had experienced it. It is a wonderful illustration of the unpredictability of the creative impulse that this desperately unhappy woman, so given to a solemn, highflown rhetoric of human brotherhood, in and out of her novels, should have demonstrated her real gifts of sympathy and understanding, her real seriousness if you like, in those passages of broad, shameless farce which help so much to make *The Story of an African Farm* still a living book today.

*

Olive Schreiner's first, adolescent attempt at a novel, *Undine*, was for the most part set in England: a never-never England taken entirely from books, where, when the characters are not drinking tea on the lawn or walking through vaguely described woods, the snow is incessantly falling. From the hundreds of pages of *Undine* devoted to that fantasy-land we can judge just how difficult it was for her to make plausible to herself the material she knew at first hand as a source of fiction: her snow-less, wood-less, lawn-less Karroo, about which not a word had ever appeared in any novel. (A number of fifth-rate adventure stories set in South Africa had begun to appear in England in the second half of the nineteenth century. Many, if not all of them, seem to have been written by people who did an Olive-Schreiner-in-reverse, as it were: they wrote about the Cape and its exotic peoples, beasts, and landscapes without ever having seen them.) To anyone who reflects seriously on what it must be like to grow up within a society that had never been given a voice of its own, there must appear something almost heroic about the opening of *The Story of an African Farm*, with its first fine sentence: 'The full African moon poured down its light from the blue sky into the wide, lonely plain . . .' and its description of the kopje near the homestead, the sheep kraals, the Kaffir huts, and Tant' Sannie, the Boer housewife, in bed, in her clothes, dreaming of the sheep's trotters she had eaten for supper that night. 'She dreamed that one stuck fast in her throat, and she rolled her huge form from side to side, and snorted horribly.'

The African moon, by the way, *is* bright enough to fill the sky with a hard blue radiance; the sentence I have quoted is not an inaccurate one. Which suggests another way of conveying the initial difficulty Olive Schreiner had to overcome as a novelist. When I read her novel for the first time, some sixty years after it was first published, I had to struggle with my own incredulity that the kopjes, kraals and cactus plants she mentions were of the same kind as those I was familiar with; so little experience had I had of encountering them within the pages of a book. For it is not only the hitherto undescribed, uncelebrated, wordless quality of the life around him that makes it seem implausible to the colonial as a fit subject for fiction: it is also (no matter how bright the moonlight may be) its appearance of drabness, its thinness, its lack of richness and variety in comparison with what he has read about in the books that come to him from abroad. So much so, that when a writer from such a society presents it as simply bursting with 'life' and 'colour' one must suspect him of having chosen to see it from without, as his metropolitan readers would want to see it, and not as he himself has experienced it. It is not accidental that in her introduction to the second edition of the book, Olive Schreiner used the metaphor of squeezing the colours from her brush and dipping it into the grey pigments around her.

This is not to deny that *The Story of an African Farm* is in many respects, some of them damaging to it, a very 'literary' piece of work; the fruit in places more of reading than of life. It could hardly be otherwise. Even Bonaparte Blenkins – tramp, rogue, sadist and comic, one of the liveliest of the novel's inventions – owes much to other books. Sometimes he talks like Mr Jingle of *The Pickwick Papers*; sometimes he preaches like Mr Chadband of *Bleak House*. As for Lyndall, the doomed, imperious heroine, who goes through the novel complaining that her heart is dead, that she is incapable of feeling, but who is shown to us as never finding anyone worthy of her own high emotions – she, too, is not an unfamiliar figure to any reader of Victorian fiction. The portentous loquacity of Lyndall's feminist convictions is more of a novelty; but it can be an entirely welcome one only to those readers (of whom there are of course always bound to be some) who look to fiction simply to make them feel more secure in the views they already hold. Even such readers, though, should be given pause by the unconscious intensity with which the author in effect persecutes Lyndall for being what every girl might wish to be: so beautiful, so eloquent, so utterly irresistible to men and so disdainful of them. And there is no need to dwell unkindly on the second-hand lyricism of such chapters as the interlude, 'Times and Seasons', describing the growth of a child's consciousness, or Waldo's meeting with the stranger.

Altogether, the faults of the book are glaring, and it would be pointless to try to gloss over them. But it would be even more of a mistake to allow the faults to obscure the novel's considerable merits. Essentially the story is one of two girls, two cousins, who grow up on a Karroo farm, under the slovenly guardianship of a fat Boer woman. One of the girls is obedient, kindhearted, domesticated, a born housewife; the other is proud, restless, rebellious, intellectually avid. By the end of the book, Lyndall, the rebel, is dead, after having given birth to an illegitimate child; the other girl, Em, is about to marry a young man who will never love her as she loves him, because his heart – and, in one peculiarly revelatory, dreamlike episode of transvestism, his manhood itself – had been given to the unattainable Lyndall. The remaining characters, apart from Tant' Sannie, are the devout, childlike German overseer of the farm; Waldo, his son, who shares some of Lyndall's intellectual curiosity and hatred of received opinions, but has none of her fierceness; and the redoubtable Bonaparte Blenkins, the ragged crook and confidence man, who comes by chance to the farm, and whose attempt to drive Waldo's father from it is foiled only by the old man's death. Waldo comes back to the farm to die too, after having travelled about the country without ever learning just what he had been looking for. Those who seek and strive are killed off; the others survive.*

Two grounds for my admiration of the novel I have already given: its passages of comedy, which are often outrightly farcical, and none the worse in my opinion for being so; and the power and originality of its evocation of the Karroo landscapes the author knew so well. But there is another, which – given what we know of Olive Schreiner's life and temperament, her extreme youth when she wrote the book, and the urgency of the passions she poured into it – is almost as surprising as the comic spirit it displays. That quality I would describe as the book's calmness. She manages to display repeatedly a degree of disinterestedness towards her own characters which is the mark of the true novelist: a readiness not

* *From Man to Man* is also built around the lives of two girls – two sisters this time – who grow up together on an up-country farm. But it shows an interesting and rather more subtle variation of the pattern adumbrated in the earlier novel. In *From Man to Man* it is the intellectual, feminist sister who becomes a housewife and mother, and remains one, however unhappily; whereas the obliging, simple-minded, home-loving girl is seduced by her tutor, then rejected by her fiancé when he learns of that lapse, then carried away to London . . . Ultimately the author's plan was that she was to end up as an outright prostitute; but that section of the novel was never written.

to bear grudges against them; to allow them to develop or change (and change back again to what they were before); to let the events of the novel make their own impersonal comment, as it were, upon what the people do or say. I am not speaking here merely of charity on the part of the writer towards her own characters; but of something harder to achieve, beyond either charity or animus. Thus there is nothing clownish about Bonaparte when he flogs Waldo in one of the most disturbing scenes in the book. But his cruelty does not transform him into a wholly villainous figure; just as in the later slapstick of his humiliation, when a barrel of pickled meat is poured over him, there is still a touch of pathos:

'You see, the water was fatty, and that has made all the sand stick to me, and my hair,' said Bonaparte, tenderly touching the little fringe at the back of his head, 'is all caked over like a little plank: you wouldn't think it was hair at all.'

Tant' Sannie is credulous, sensual, lazy, and ready to acquiesce in every one of Bonaparte's cruelties; but she is also – what she is; and at the end of the book we see her telling Emily how to boil soap, and fondly wishing her as many children in five years as a cow has calves.

There is one further small example of the author's creative detachment I would like to mention. *The Story of an African Farm* is about the white people on the farm, not the black; it is far from being the novel of 'race relations' which many people have come to expect every South African novel to be. The black people in it are merely extras, supernumeraries, part of the background. But in one brief scene we are made aware of the possibilities that such a background can contain. When Tant' Sannie drives Waldo's father off the farm because of the lies Bonaparte has told about him, the old German turns in bewilderment to her coloured maid:

She was his friend; she would tell him kindly the truth.
The woman answered with a ringing laugh.
'Give it him, old missus! Give it him!'
It was so nice to see the white man who had been master hunted down. The coloured woman laughed and threw a dozen mealie grains into her mouth to chew.

The servant is not deflected from her pleasure by the fact that of all the people on the farm, the old man had always been the most tender-hearted to black and white alike. Nor is Olive Schreiner deflected by the pleasure or pain of either from her pursuit of the truth.

Creative detachment? Creative immersion might be a better phrase to describe so complex a mode of artistic apprehension. Only in *The Story of an African Farm* was she capable of it for long enough to bring the work, however flawed it might be, to a conclusion. Neither her own unhappiness, nor her quasi-religious insistence that such unhappiness somehow be exorcised from the experience of all mankind, ever permitted it to happen again.

*

In 1913 Olive Schreiner came once again to England. She had paid two previous visits to it, after her return to South Africa; both had been brief and of little consequence. Now she was to remain there for seven years, practically until the end of her life. She came alone, without her husband; and again she began the round of boarding-houses and rented rooms, of visits to doctors, and of attendance at sundry meetings. But there were differences. She was an old woman now, not a young one. She had no hope of ever being able to finish her novel, and no energy to attempt writing of any other kind. Her reputation had faded, and people no longer sought her out. Four of the seven years of her stay were those of the First World War; in the hysteria of the time she suffered both because of her German-sounding name and because of her pacifist convictions. (Most of the meetings she attended were held in protest against the war.) Her physical health, as ever, was poor; and her state of mind, in the words of one of her biographers, 'was undoubtedly very difficult'. A young woman who visited her has left a picture of her sitting in the Holborn Restaurant, dressed in 'a bottle-green coat and skirt, without pretence of fashion and distinctive style; and a hat that left me gasping, because it was a fussy arrangement of straw and lace and (I think) battered roses.' The same young woman remarked that there was 'a bitterness' in her freethinking.

The letters she wrote conscientiously to her husband throughout the whole seven years tell the story in their own way. Though they are without the frenzy of those she had written thirty-five years before – or perhaps for that very reason – they make much sadder reading.

> I have no news to give you; have seen no-one and heard nothing but what is in the papers. This morning I felt I must get out of my room or something would happen to me; so, in fog and warm, sweating, misty rain, I went to Edgware Road and got a bus that goes to Hampstead . . .

> I have so longed during the last months just once to feel happy again; and now I am happy when I remember that dream. It was only a dream, but I had the sensation of happiness which I would have had if it were real . . . [About a dream in which she walked in a field in the countryside, and was treated affectionately by the animals in it.]

> It's ten days since I've spoken to anyone except the girl who brings in the coals . . .

> I don't think absolute solitude is healthy for any human creature.

Finally, in 1920 her husband joined her; within weeks of his arrival she had sailed, on her own, for the Cape once more. She died a few months later, in her sleep, in a Cape Town boarding-house.

The influence of her work on the South African writers in English who have followed her has been an enduring one. In the nature of the case it was bound to be so, for nothing can take from her the honour of being the first to make usable the country and the people within it as a subject for fiction. Those who have followed her, no matter how different their approaches or styles of thinking and feeling, have had the encouragement of knowing the field to be not entirely barren; what is more, they have seen in her work an example of how natural, how direct, how free of the burden of self-consciousness, it is possible to be in presenting their country, with its particular cultural atmosphere – or lack of atmosphere. Most of the English-language writers of fiction since her day, it is true, have been all but exclusively preoccupied with the relations between white and black, a subject on which she touched only tangentially in *The Story of an African Farm*. But that does not affect the issue; or the size of our debt to her.

SIXTEEN

YIDDISH FICTION IN SOUTH AFRICA

◆

The little *dorp* of Kenhardt lies in the north western corner of the Cape Province, one of the least populated regions of the Republic: on the edge of the Kalahari desert, as people are inclined to say (in rather random fashion) about such places. In 1914 the present writer's father, H.M. Jacobson, rode on horseback through Kenhardt as a member of a commando of 'loyalist' Boers from the Eastern Transvaal; they were in pursuit of another commando headed by General Maritz, who had gone into rebellion against the Pretoria government on the outbreak of the First World War. In his partial autobiography, *My Early Days*, sections of which have been published in magazines in South Africa and England, my father tells the following anecdote:

> When our commando rode into Kenhardt I noticed a building that looked uncommonly like a small synagogue. I broke ranks and approached it a little closer. I was not mistaken. I have a vivid recollection of the incident for two reasons. Firstly I was reprimanded by the commandant for breaking ranks when riding through the town. And secondly, when I looked at the foundation stone, I noticed an error in the Hebrew spelling in the engraving. The word 'Even' (stone) was spelt with the letter *ayin* instead of with an *aleph*. I pointed this out to the head of the congregation when I later had lunch with him – something I would *not* do now.

What is most remarkable about this story, I would suggest, is not that my father, who had migrated from Eastern Europe to South Africa in 1903, and who had been farming in the Lichtenberg district when the war broke out, should have been a member of a Boer commando. Nor is it the fact that barely ten years after the end of the Anglo-Boer War, Afrikaners should have been in armed conflict with their fellow-Afrikaners. It is rather that *Kenhardt*, of all places, should at that date have had a sufficiently large Jewish community to warrant the establishment and maintenance of a synagogue – even if it was one whose founders were unsure of how to spell a common Hebrew word. I have no idea whether that building is still standing; but I am certain that the community which built it has long since vanished.

The Jews of Eastern Europe began to migrate in relatively large numbers to South Africa only after the discovery of gold on the Reef at the beginning of the 1880s. Inevitably, most of them made their way to the gold or diamond fields; many remained in the well-established ports like Cape Town and Durban which served the rapidly growing cities of the interior. In addition to these, however, a significant number spread out in all directions along the rapidly expanding railway lines, and beyond them, across the length and breadth of the country: a pattern of movement strikingly unlike that of their cousins who had gone to the United States, say, or to England. These newcomers set themselves up in business as itinerant merchants (*smouses*) or village shopkeepers, or first as the one, then as the other; some became cattle speculators, farmers, hoteliers. As recently as the 1940s, when I travelled as a boy with my family on holiday journeys across the country, it sometimes seemed to me that there was no place so small and remote as to be without its Jewish family or families. One saw their names on sun-blistered shop-awnings or on bright brass plates affixed to tiny offices; the heads of such families, when one met them, generally turned out to be small, rather hardbitten, unillusioned men, speaking a strange Yiddish-like Afrikaans or Afrikaans-like Yiddish; their children, by contrast, were English-speaking, defensive about their 'backveld' origins, and eager to urbanise themselves.

Well, they succeeded. If the first phase of the community's growth, roughly speaking, was one of immigration and dispersion, the second was that of consolidation and concentration. The Jews of the *platteland* began to move to the cities largely in search of material self-betterment: for the same reason, ultimately, that the Afrikaners were to do so, in incomparably greater numbers, and the blacks in even greater numbers still, in subsequent decades. Indeed, by the 60s smaller cities like Kimberley and Bloemfontein, which had themselves been magnets to the Jews of their hinterland, had begun to lose their communities to the larger centres. There were of course peculiarly 'ethnic' reasons, too, for this movement: not just the celebrated eagerness of the members of the second generation to enter their favoured professions (medicine, the law) for which wider opportunities were to be found in the cities, but also the feeling that Jewish religious, social, and cultural institutions could be more easily preserved there. The internal migration was also hastened by the adoption of avowedly anti-Semitic policies by the Afrikaner Nationalist Party during the 1930s and 40s: a development which did much to envenom relations between the Jews in the countryside and their neighbours.

The third phase of the community's history – the present one – has followed ineluctably from the others. It can best be described as one of attrition from within; this as a consequence of intermarriage, emigration (in the face of political dangers and uncertainties ahead), and a rapidly declining birthrate. Nevertheless, even today the Jews of South Africa continue to play a role out of proportion to their numbers in the country's financial, industrial, and professional life. This would hardly be disputed both by those who are well-disposed to them and by those who are not. As one might expect, South African Jews have also been prominent beyond their numbers in fostering the country's artistic and intellectual traditions.

As far as literature is concerned, the Jewish contribution has been made almost entirely in the English language and through the institutions of the English-speaking section of the population. (Though there are a few names which occupy prominent places in the history of Afrikaans literature; and the efforts of some Jewish writers and producers have been important to the emergence of black theatre groups in recent years.) Recently, the labours of Joseph Sherman of Witwatersrand University, Johannesburg, have revealed that a distinctively South African genre of stories in the Yiddish language also began to emerge at a very early stage of the period of mass migration from Eastern Europe. Now that some of those stories have been made accessible to readers of English (in an anthology edited by Joseph Sherman and entitled *From a Land Far Off*) they too can for the first time become part of a common South African patrimony.

*

In his introduction to the anthology, its editor summarises the history of Yiddish as a spoken and written language from the time of its origins (chiefly out of Middle High German) onwards. He also describes the attempts that certain writers and publicists made in Europe during the nineteenth century to redeem it from its status as a despised 'jargon', a kind of depraved, Hebraised dialect of German, and to have it recognised as a language as worthy of respect as any other, in which high literary and intellectual ambitions could be realised. (No South African can escape drawing the parallel here with Afrikaans, which also had to fight vigorous battles for acceptance as a serious language, so to speak, and as an indispensable element of the national consciousness of the Afrikaner people.) Anyone who tells the story of Yiddish has then to go on to speak of its end as a living language, which was brought about by a single historical event: the destruction of the Jewry of Eastern Europe at the hands of the Nazis.

Many of the Yiddish writers in South Africa did their work before the onset of the great crisis which overwhelmed their kinsmen in Europe; some of them wrote during it; some were left to memorialise what had been lost, in the aftermath. The anthology, however, is confined to stories they wrote about the new land, 'Africa', as they simply called it, and which were published in a variety of hopelessly short-lived journals which they themselves battled to bring into existence. As writers of the first phase of the community's history (even when they did their work in later years, retrospectively) their prime topic was bound to be the vicissitudes of immigrant life. They describe the country itself, with its bareness, its space, its relative emptiness, its abrupt, desultory cities; more intensely still, they try to describe the encounters between the immigrants and the cultures and peoples with which they were confronted.

The stories show such encounters often to have been abrasive, charged with hostility and suspicion on both sides. This should not come as a surprise. What is more surprising, perhaps, is that the writers so often speak of their immigrant Jewish characters somehow recognising themselves in the apparently alien folk among whom their lot had been cast. Initially, at least, there is a tendency to see the Afrikaners as a godfearing, hospitable, quasi-Israelite people, themselves wandering in search of their promised land. This not wholly romanticised view of an earlier phase of Afrikaner society is strongly reminiscent of that adopted by certain English-language writers – like Pauline Smith, for example, in the stories gathered in *The Little Karroo*. With the blacks there is a mirroring of a different kind. Though they, of all groups, are most 'native' to the country, they are described by some of the writers as fellow-migrants, too; people who are summoned from afar to serve the commerce, industry, and domestic establishments of white society and yet thrust contemptuously into its margins. Bewildered, dislocated, outcast and yet indispensable, unable to comprehend the languages in which they are addressed, they are sometimes to be pitied, sometimes to be feared, always to be regarded with a kind of uneasy wonder, in which recognition struggles with a profound unfamiliarity. The English-speaking South Africans, interestingly enough, hardly appear in the tales. Perhaps their social and cultural dominance at the time simply made them too daunting, or too remote, a group for these authors to tackle.

On the whole the Jewish immigrants to South Africa were as proverty-stricken when they arrived as their cousins who crowded into New York's Lower East Side and the East End of London; they had to take jobs which no one else wanted; the political and economic insecurities of the country were often more starkly apparent to them than the opportunities of which they had heard in the old country. Nowhere in the two dozen stories reprinted in *From a Land Far Off* is the lot of the newcomer sentimentalised. On the contrary, a reader may well come to feel by the end of the volume that he has learned rather more than he wishes to know about the nomadic life of the pedlar, say, or the noisy, sweaty, smelly job of the 'kaffireatnik', the assistant in the eating-houses for black mine-workers. ('Kaffireaters', these institutions were elegantly termed; hence 'kaffireatnik'.) However, there is another reason why the theme of failure looms as large in the anthology as it does. As far as the writers are concerned, the story *is* one of failure. The immigrants, or many of them, may eventually have prospered, but in so doing they and their children are described as having lost their most valuable and distinctive possession: their Jewishness, at least as the writers would wish the term to be understood. That loss, which encompasses the strict observance of their religion, as well as the languages they had brought with them (Yiddish, and the sacred tongue, Hebrew), could not be compensated for, the stories insist in their different ways, by any material advantage that may have accrued in the process.

Within this general plaintive or accusatory account of things one can sometimes pick up the sound of a complaint which is never actually expressed: that issuing from the story-teller who feels his audience, small though it is, to be turning away from him and his medium even as he speaks to it. One also notices that while the stories lament the decline of the traditional pieties, their authors show themselves to have a receptive eye for villainy and disreputable behaviour; their relish for these is rather like that which some Yiddish writers in Eastern Europe had for the kinds of Jewish gangsterism best known to them. (One thinks also of Isaac Babel, with his tales of Benya Krik and the Jewish hoodlums of Odessa.) The life depicted in the anthology is not at all genteel: fighting, drinking, irregular unions with black and Afrikaner women, and plain cheating and sharp business practice are all represented in it; not to speak of what one writer refers to as 'some judicious arson'. One cannot help suspecting, indeed, that precisely because they were confident their stories would be read only by readers and speakers of Yiddish like themselves, the authors permitted themselves to speak more frankly about such aspects of immigrant life than they might otherwise have done.

Are the stories then to be valued primarily as documents, rather than as literary works? The answer is that this distinction is itself a misleading one. The stories would only doubtfully have merit as documents if they did not move and entertain the reader as imaginative writing is supposed to. Some are amateurish, certainly; hardly more than little homilies or appeals for sympathy. But at their best they do have a genuine literary power: by which I mean that the world perceived or presented in them is not ultimately separable from the characters who perceive it. In such stories the perception *is* or becomes the character, and vice versa.

Take, for instance, the portrait of the nameless horse belonging to Mendel, a hawker of fruit and vegetables, from the story 'Who Comes First' by Hyman Polsky.

True, it had a cataract over the left eye, dripped urine continually, and was always surrounded by hordes of green flies; it had collapsed sides, protruding bones and well-worn knees . . . nevertheless it was a good horse: quietly and sedately it did the work, contented with its lot. It did not complain when it had to stand a few hours longer in the shafts, or had sometimes to fast a little. Apparently the clever horse knew that its master was not himself given strongly to eating . . . When Mendel arrived home in the evenings and the horse, covered in sweat, stood as if dead from exhaustion, Chaya-Yente felt enormous compassion for it. If it had been at all possible she would, it seems, have taken it into the house and given it a little glass of tea, in the same way as – to make a distinction between sacred and profane things mentioned successively – her husband. But because she could not, she would fiddle about him, pat him, stroke him, look him in the eye and speak friendly words. The horse, it turned out, well understood, because at such times it would lift up its head as if to say, 'What use are all these things? Rather give me something to eat.'

Or this account, from 'Ben' by J.M. Sherman, of a lonely storekeeper's Sunday morning in the countryside: a passage which, like many others in the anthology, reveals the depth of the writer's debt to his Russian exemplars. In this case it is Gogol, perhaps, who is most likely to come to mind.

On Sundays he smartened himself up. On Sunday he generally gave a good deal of time to himself . . . He would lie in bed and read the *Sunday Times*. Later, walking around in his pyjamas in summer with a flyswatter in his hand he used to chase the flies from his room for half an hour, and in winter, sitting in the small kitchen which was built on to his bedroom, he used to throw coals into the small iron stove, and each time say to himself, 'Cold!' Still later he took a bath, shaved, cut off his corn, trimmed the hair from his ears and nose . . . When he had done all this he locked himself in his bedroom and prayed. From a drawer he pulled out a faded pair of phylacteries, with peeling, nearly white straps, and contemplated them with the expression of one who was seeing them for the first time . . . What he said there nobody knew: he had no prayer book. After ten or fifteen minutes he would turn sharply to face the bed, spit three times, as he might have done anywhere, snatch off the phylacteries, pack them back in the yellow, Springbok tobacco bag from which he had taken them, and hide them in the drawer – until the next Sunday.

*

'Documentary' in quite another and unambiguous sense are the biographies of individual writers with which the editor has prefaced each group of stories. These make up a sub-genre of their own, with their tales of overweening ambitions poured into Lilliputian furores; of fiercely nurtured and now wholly forgotten political and personal differences (Zionist versus leftist, Hebraist versus Yiddishist, patron versus client); of unavailing struggles to keep journals alive in the face of tiny circulations and preposterous finances. How admirable, how poignant, and how risible, somehow, is the picture of a shopkeeper stuck in a place like De Aar, that most forlorn of railway junctions, in the middle of the endless, sun-blighted Karroo, who is painstakingly putting together a volume of verse in Yiddish, for eventual publication back in Poland; or the picture of a moneyless handful of people launching a Yiddish journal in Bloemfontein – once the tinpot capital of the Boer Republic of the Orange Free State; now merely a provincial capital – under the resounding title, *Freistater Beginen. The Free State Dawn*: nothing less.

A somewhat similar source of pathos and amusement can be found in the glossary at the back of the book, which is much more than the dry compilation it might ordinarily be assumed to be. So improbable a collocation of words and phrases from Yiddish, Hebrew, Zulu, Xhosa, Afrikaans, and broken English in itself encapsulates the nature of the extraordinary enterprise in which these Yiddish writers were engaged; it reveals the yawning racial and cultural disjunctions their work confronted, embodied, and attempted to bridge. Where else could one possibly find in such proximity words and phrases like *gefilte fish* (Yid., stuffed fish) and *bhansela* (zulu, small present), *Kiddush* (Heb., blessing) and *Nagmaal* (Afr., Holy Communion), *xoxo* (Xhosa, insect), and *Yahrzeit* (Yid., prayers for the dead), *fiktses* (Eng., fixtures), *shofar* (Heb., ram's horn trumpet), *bokjôl* (Afr., country dance), and all the rest?

Which brings me directly to my last point; one which is not comic in any sense. Some paragraphs earlier I referred to 'a common patrimony' which might be thought to be available to the peoples of South Africa. Given the country's past, present, and likely future, this phrase must have been taken by many readers to be no more than a sentimental or pious flourish. That is not how I would wish it to be read, however. What I had in mind was something specific and yet difficult to define. If one can discern anything resembling a common cultural patrimony in South Africa, it is to be found, painfully enough, in the dislocations and disruptions which each group inflicts on the others and is provoked by them to feel within itself. The liveliest and most distinctive elements in the cultural self-consciousness of the country are by their very nature interstitial and reactive. They grow at the point where mutually hostile and mutually dependent racial and linguistic groups meet; though they are indeed painful, they are often very funny too. In describing a developing self-consciousness of this kind it is impossible to tell abrasion from stimulus, threat from nurture. But each group, willy-nilly, recognises its own perplexities and predicaments in the terms that the others have managed to articulate; and recoils from them; and in so doing creates them anew.

According to official doctrine, of course, a 'true' culture emerges only out of a jealously preserved separateness between peoples, each of which knows itself *as* a people only so far as it manages to keep itself inviolate from mingling or even, ideally, from contact with others. But official doctrine, which has for decades been attempting to impose by force its own versions of political and cultural separateness on the variegated groups who make up the country, is false to the deepest experience even of those who invented it. Who can doubt that Afrikaner nationalism, in all its manifestations, is itself a reactive movement? And who can doubt that the same is true of those burgeoning black consciousness movements which are today so loudly proclaiming their indifference or hostility to the white man and his works?

Many of the Yiddish writers whose stories appear in *From a Land Far Off* cherished their own variety of the myth of a lost, 'pure' culture, forever private to themselves. There is no such thing: certainly not in South Africa; probably nowhere else either. It is appropriate that a volume lovingly translated from a lost language should serve to remind us of this truth.

SEVENTEEN

THE KING AND I

An excessive interest in the Old Testament, Evelyn Waugh once remarked, is often a sign of incipient insanity. His opinion seems to be widely shared, to judge from the way people looked at me when I told them I was writing a novel based on the story of the rape of King David's daughter, Tamar. Admittedly, I knew, and they did not, that the novel was intended to be neither a 'Biblical Epic' in the style of Cecil B. de Mille, nor a painstaking, naturalistic attempt to recreate the period in which it was set. On the contrary. One of the things that strongly attracted me to the subject was the chance it gave me to break away sharply from the conventions of naturalism in narrative technique and in mode of approach to times past as well as times present.

The Rape of Tamar was published in due course, and on the whole was well received by reviewers and by the readers it found. And by my relieved friends. Subsequently I asked one of them, who had shown some alarm beforehand, if he would have responded in the same fashion if I had told him that I was working on a story adapted from the Greek legends. He replied stoutly yes, he would have. But this assertion did not altogether convince me. The relationship which both believers and non-believers have to the Bible is obviously quite unlike that which they have to the Greek legends. Nothing has been more important to the shaping of the society we live in than a belief in the veracity of the Hebrew and Christian scriptures; nothing, that is, other than a disbelief in their veracity.

My own interest in the story related in 2 Samuel 13 did not spring from a previously formulated ambition to write on a biblical theme. What came first was simply a fascination with the story of the rape and its consequences – which I had stumbled across some twenty years before I set about trying to write the novel. I had been led there originally by a youthfully self-conscious effort at intellectual self-improvement. Since neither of my parents were believers, the 'Jewishness' of our household had been more a social-racial inheritance than a religious one; certainly no Bible-reading had ever taken place within it. Occasional and reluctant attendance at synagogue services had done almost nothing to reduce my ignorance of the Scriptures, nor had the acquisition of those scraps of Hebrew which my father had insisted I learn. As for the knowledge I had acquired of random biblical tales and characters, and of orthodox Jewish practices, and of items of Christian dogma – all that these could do, of their very nature, was to remind me of how ill-informed I was.

So, if you want to find out about the Bible, what do you do? The answer seemed to me plain. You sit down and read it. Which I attempted to do. Like many another hopeful tyro, I thought I would begin at the beginning and go right through to the end: in the Authorised Version, needless to say. Of course I failed abjectly in the task I had set myself. The holy text yielded not illumination or inspiration, but bewilderment. True, it began, as I had done, at the very beginning; but thereafter – !

I had naïvely imagined that people became believers because of what they read in the Bible (though it was not in search of belief that I was reading it); now I realised that they read the Bible, indeed that they were able to read the Bible, because they believed. The creation myths; the tales of the patriarchs; the wars and migrations of Israel; the comminations of the prophets against their own people and all other peoples; the ritualistic details of the priestly codes and their incomprehensible building instructions; the wisdom writings, by turns so impressive and so laborious – not to speak of the Gospels, which were wholly unlike all that had gone before, and which yet claimed to be a direct consequence or denouement of it; and the Epistles of Paul, so different again; and the final cannon-shot of the Revelation – what *but* belief could bring all these into a meaningful relationship with one another?*

Anyway, in the middle of all this was the story of David's reign, told by the anonymous figure to whom scholars have given the title of Court Chronicler; and in the middle of that was the single chapter devoted to the rape. There it was, complete, from the 'sickness' of Amnon's desire for his sister to the revenge taken on him years later by the doomed Absalom. The compression of the tale, its startling reversals of direction, the truths about human nature hidden and revealed in the protagonists' terse words and violent actions – it was these that seemed worth exploring and enlarging on, for their own sake, as it were. But when, after carrying the idea in the back of my mind for decades, I did finally

---

* Ironically enough, a dozen years after the publication of *The Rape of Tamar*, I was to publish a study of the Bible entitled *The Story of the Stories*. In this book I considered both the Hebrew and Christian testaments as the carriers of precisely the kind of ever-changing yet coherent narrative they had seemed so much to lack during my first bewildered encounter with them. Nothing in my own career has surprised me more than my continuing preoccupation with the Scriptures (which is reflected also in my most recent novel, *Her Story*); especially, perhaps, as this preoccupation has not led from or towards anything a believer would call belief. What has become incomparably stronger as a result of it, though, is a conviction that every social and intellectual 'tradition' is in effect an ever-changing, never-ending 'story' told to and heard by successive generations; and that it is in attending to and participating in the telling of such overarching stories that our individual stories find much of their meaning.

challenge myself to make of it what I could, it was obviously impossible for me to perceive it in isolation either from the history that had preceded it and followed it, or from my own relationship to that history. Indeed, the disparities and implausibilities of that relationship, as I saw them, had to be incorporated in the very structure of the novel itself. Hence the anachronistic utterances of Amnon's friend and enemy, the scheming Yonadab, whom I present as the narrator of the tale: a man whom *we* summon into a ghostly form of life, as he wearily acknowledges, every time we seek to understand his motives and those of others in the drama.

I emphasise for good reason the anomalies and discomforts of the relationship to the past I was trying to write about. When I was growing up in a small South African town it did not seem very surprising to me, so far as I thought about it at all, that the Boers should have chosen to see themselves in the bleak, warlike image of the chosen people making their way through the wilderness. Reading English history, I could see why both sides in the Civil War – Cromwell's troopers and the defenders of the Lord's anointed alike – should have gone to war to the rhythms of the Authorised Version, and should have conducted many of their debates on the rights of kingship precisely in the language of the books of Samuel. Even the African sects that flourished obscurely but noisily in their areas of the town seemed entitled to claim their kinship to the Hebrew slaves awaiting their deliverance from Pharaoh. (In those days the African separatist sects were simply called the 'Zionist churches'; I do not know if that is still the case.) But that it should have been the Jewish business and professional men in the town, whose gentilities and ambitions were apparently made all the more intense by the Hitlerian horrors then taking place in Europe – that it was *they* who were the true inheritors of the clangour and passion of the Old Testament, the present-day representatives of its kings, prophets, soldiers, shepherds and all . . . what a disparity, what an implausibility, what a joke that seemed to be!

Yet it was so. It was because my father was one of them, and not a Boer or an Englishman, that I had been taught the rudiments of Hebrew as a boy. It was they who in some fashion still observed the festivals and sabbaths prescribed in the Old Testament. It was because of the straits to which their kinsfolk had been driven in Europe that a people who had compelled themselves to use the Hebrew tongue had once again begun to live in Palestine, after a lapse of more than two thousand years, and that the state of Israel was eventually to be re-established there. When I visited Israel for the first time, however, doubleness and disorientation of a similar kind to that described above were again among the reactions I had to the land itself. From one point of view, its small-scale but melodramatic topography matched everything that had been written about it; especially lofty, stony Jerusalem and the wilderness on its doorstep. From another, the gulf between reality and the extravagant claims of Scripture could never yawn more widely than when their settings were directly in front of you. You did not have to go to the well-known sites of pilgrimage to feel it. Here, for example, was the valley of Ayalon, where Joshua commanded the sun to stand still so that the defeat of the Amorites might be accomplished. It was a modest green valley, like any other, with its quota of stones, crops, trees, grass and telephone poles. Another joke! That particular joke was made more bitter by the fact that the valley had been the scene of severe fighting during the Arab-Israel war of 1948, when hundreds had died in a single day and the sun had gazed down indifferently on the proceedings and then set at its appointed time.

Where do we belong, how can we possibly find ourselves, among those ancient, small wars, those codes of conduct that have become all but incomprehensible to us, those cosmographies which we know to be nonsensical? How do the figures of the ancient world fit in among us, with our aeroplanes, newspapers, vast populations, confused relativities of judgement? Sometimes, with varying admixtures of self-pity and self-admiration, we cannot help feeling that we are absolutely marooned in our own time, it is so different from any that preceded it. But if that is so, why can these apparently distant people from the past suddenly seem so close to us? Why is the tether that ties us to them so short?

How short? The length of a sentence, that's all! Amnon's feelings towards Tamar after the rape: 'The hatred with which he hated her was greater than the love with which he had loved her.' Tamar's reponse to her brutal expulsion from his house: 'This wrong in sending me away is greater than the other which you did to me.' And Absalom when he hears what has happened: 'But Absalom spoke to Amnon neither good nor bad; for Absalom hated Amnon, because he had forced his sister.'

If this is true of what is actually said by some of these antique heroes and villains, it is true also that the obscurity which surrounds them can itself become, paradoxically, a mode of revelation. They emerge slowly into clarity, if we allow them to, rather as the patterning of our own lives and motives can belatedly become known to us. The appearance of David himself – the man without whom there would have been no united kingdom of Israel and Judah; no capital city in Jerusalem; no place for the Ark of the Lord to come to rest in, and therefore no place for the memories of his people to refer to; no restive and rebellious princes, and certainly no court historian to record his reign in such detail – is a case in point. Initially he appears to be almost wholly a figure of legend and myth. His story repeats itself and directly contradicts itself. At one moment he is made known to his predecessor, Saul, through the killing of the Philistine giant (a feat ascribed elsewhere to other Israelite heroes); then he comes to the court as the winner of a sort of primitive talent contest, when a search is made for a musician who will soothe the king during his fits of melancholy; then he is chosen to be king by Samuel himself, while he is tending his father's sheep outside Bethlehem. Similar repetitions and contradictions mark the accounts of his flight from Saul to the caves of Adullam and his subsequent career as a rebel and guerilla chieftain.

Yet by the time one comes to the matters covered in the court history, it is impossible to resist the belief that one is confronting a recognisable historical figure. The reaches and mutual interpenetrations of the king's guile and piety, generosity and ruthlessness, sagacity and self-ignorance, are inexhaustible. So is his capacity to hold them together through some deep principle of character, which is shown to have had a touching and awe-inspiring effect on those around him, his enemies included. And if it is said that all this may have nothing to do with historical 'fact', but is merely an expression of the literary skill of the chronicler, then the case I am making is affected not at all; if anything it is strengthened. Then one can only wonder all the more at this writer's capacity to reveal to us so much of ourselves, across so many centuries and what we would imagine to be such profound changes in outlook and belief. It is the anonymous chronicler, then, who is our contemporary; who knows us and our tender-hearted tyrants, our loving and oppressive fathers, our merciless friends and erratically forgiving enemies, better than we know ourselves.

Not long after finishing *The Rape of Tamar* I was told by the late Yigael Yadin, the most famous of Israeli archaeologists, the 'conqueror' of Masada and Hazor, that there is not a single shred of supporting evidence from archaeological sources that David ever actually existed; this notwithstanding the detail with which his reign is described in the biblical chronicle. (Even his name may not have been a 'name' at all, but rather a generic title found all over the ancient Near East for a leader or commander of men; perhaps even a demigod.) In point of fact the biblical text actually informs us that David was not a builder – it says, in characteristic fashion, that he was explicitly forbidden by God to build – so it should not really surprise us that nothing of him, other than the frail, written word of his chronicles, has survived. But that has been sufficient.

A few pages above I mentioned my childhood in South Africa to illustrate the tortuousness with which our continuities with the past are likely to manifest themselves. It was only when *The Rape of Tamar* was done that I realised it was not only as a Jew but also as a South African that I had presumed to feel a special affinity with some aspects of the story of David. Why as a South African? Well, in relation to the empires and metropolitan powers of his time, he was a provincial, a man on the margins. Yet, thirty centuries later, it was his life, not that of any of the greater kings contemporary with him, which was still feeding my own fantasies, let alone those of Boers, Englishmen, Africans and innumerable others. The little kingdom he established lasted only a few decades before it fell into disorder and came under the hegemony of recrudescent powers in the east. In terms of power of another kind, that had turned out to matter far less than one might have supposed.

ACKNOWLEDGEMENTS AND
BIBLIOGRAPHY

———◆———

[Names of books which occasioned an article or review are given with publisher, place of origin, and date. The journals to which I am indebted for the first appearance of essays or parts of essays are also cited. Sources of quotations not identified within the text are listed in abbreviated form; so are other titles discussed. Books mentioned incidentally and 'standard' texts (*Othello*, *Buddenbrooks*, the Bible etc.) are excluded.]

1.) and 2.) Versions of these two essays were originally given as papers at the History of Ideas Unit, Research School of Social Sciences, Australian National University, Canberra. 'Fantasy and Ethics' was subsequently published in *The Critical Review*; and 'Adult Pleasures', under a different title, in *Quadrant*. The first has since been rewritten; the latter has been wholly recast. In the process some material from another essay, 'The New Philistinism', published in *Commentary*, has been incorporated in it.

Thomas Rymer: *Critical Works* edited by C.A. Zimansky (New Haven 1956).

T.S. Eliot on 'The Waste Land': *'The Waste Land': A Facsimile and Transcript'* edited by Valerie Eliot (London 1971).

T.S. Eliot on 'sensibility': Essay on Johnson's Satires in *Selected Prose* edited by John Hayward (London 1953).

3.) This 'Note' has not been published before.

4.) An expanded version of an essay published in *The New Review*.

The Coleridge reference is taken from his poem 'To William Wordsworth' (1806).

F.R. Leavis: *The Living Principle* (London 1975).

5.) An expanded version of a review, in *The London Review of Books*, of Robert

141

Blake's *Disraeli's Grand Tour: Benjamin Disraeli and the Holy Land 1830–31* (Weidenfeld & Nicolson, London 1982).

Disraeli on 'community' and 'aggregation': *Sybil* (1845). (*Tancred* [1847] offers a similarly contrasted pair of terms: 'nation' and 'crowd'.)

Disraeli on 'reality of existence': *Coningsby* (1844).

Wordsworth: *The Prelude: Book One* (1805 version).

6.) An expanded version of a review, in *Commentary*, of Amos Elon's *Herzl* (Holt, Rinehart & Winston, New York 1975). The quotations from Herzl's diaries are taken from *The Complete Diaries of Theodore Herzl* edited by Raphael Patai and translated by Harry Zohn (New York 1960).

7.) First published in *Grand Street*.

Q.D. Leavis: 'A Fresh Approach to *Wuthering Heights*' in *Lectures in America* by F.R. and Q.D. Leavis (London 1969).

8.) Material has been taken from reviews of the following books:

Tolstoy's Letters: Volumes 1 and 2 edited and translated by R.F. Christian (The Athlone Press, London 1978) – *The Times Literary Supplement*.

Tolstoy by Henri Troyat (W.H. Allen, London 1969), translated by Nancy Amphoux – *The Guardian*.

The Last Years of Leo Tolstoy by Valentin Bulgakov (Hamish Hamilton, London 1971), translated by Ann Dunnigan – *The Guardian*.

Tolstoy Remembered by Tatyana Tolstoy (Michael Joseph, London 1971), translated by Derek Coltman – *The Guardian*.

The quotations from Tolstoy's diaries are from *Last Diaries* edited by Leon Stillman and translated by Lydia Weston Keisch (New York 1960). The revised edition of Aylmer Maude's *Life of Tolstoy* was published in London in 1930.

D.H. Lawrence: 'Morality and the Novel', reprinted in *Phoenix* (London 1961).

9.) Adapted from a review, in *The Listener*, of Isaac Babel's *You Must Know Everything: Stories 1915–37* (Jonathan Cape, London 1970), translated by Max Hayward. All other stories by Babel referred to in the essay are to be found in *Collected Stories*, translated by Walter Morison *et al.* (Harmondsworth 1961). The fragments of his wartime diary appear in *Isaac Babel: Forgotten Prose*, translated by Nicholas Stroud (Ann Arbor 1978).

Babel's references to Tolstoy are taken from an interview reprinted in *You Must Know Everything*. His description of Kipling's prose appears in the second volume of Konstantin Paustovsky's autobiography, *Years of Hope*, translated by Manya Harari and Andrew Thomson (London 1968).

10.) Adapted from a review, in *The Listener*, of Nadezhda Mandelstam's *Hope Against Hope*, translated by Max Hayward (Collins, London 1971). The same author's *Hope Abandoned*, also translated by Max Hayward, was published in London in 1974.

The discussion of Osip Mandelstam's writings refers to:

Selected Prose translated by Clarence Brown (Princeton 1966).

Selected Poems translated by Clarence Brown and W.S. Merwin (London 1973).

11.) Adapted from an article, published in *Commentary*, about several prison books – among them Sinyavsky's *A Voice from the Chorus*, translated by Kyril Fitzlyon and Max Hayward (Farrar Straus & Giroux, New York 1976); Edward Kuznetsov's *Prison Diaries*, translated by Howard Spier (Vallentine Mitchell, London 1975); Hugh Lewin's *Bandiet* (Penguin Books, Harmondsworth 1975); and the first two volumes of Alexander Solzhenitsyn's *The Gulag Archipelago* translated by H.T. Willetts (Collins, London 1974 and 75). The English translation of the final volume of *The Gulag Archipelago* appeared in 1978.

The other works by Sinyavsky referred to in the essay are:

The Trial Begins translated by Max Hayward (London 1960).

The Icicle, translated by Max Hayward and Ronald Hingley (London 1963).

The Makepeace Experiment, translated by Manya Harari (London 1965).

'The Literary Process in Russia', translated by Michael Glenny, from *Kontinent* (New York 1976).

The quotation from Isaac Rosenberg is taken from *Collected Poems* edited by D.W. Harding and Ian Parsons (London 1949).

12.) First published in *Grand Street*.

The opening paragraphs have been adapted from an article, 'D.H. Lawrence and Modern Society', which appeared in *The Journal of Contemporary History*. A few lines have also been taken from a review, in *The London Review of Books*, of Lawrence's *Collected Letters: Volume One*, edited by James Boulton (Cambridge University Press, Cambridge 1979).

The quotations on pp. 94-5 are all from *Aaron's Rod*, except for the last, which is from an essay, 'Surgery for the Novel – or a Bomb', reprinted in *Phoenix* (London 1961). The quotation on p. 98 is from 'Morality and the Novel', *op. cit.*

13.) Adapted from a review of D.H. Lasrence's *Apocalypse and the Writings on Revelation*, edited by Mara Kalnins (Cambridge University Press, Cambridge 1980), which appeared in *The London Review of Books*.

14.) This article was first published in *The London Review of Books*.

15.) A revised version of the Introduction to the Penguin English Library edition of Olive Schreiner's *The Story of an African Farm*. The quotations from her letters are taken from *Collected Letters* edited by Cronwright Schreiner (London 1924).

The biographies consulted include *The Life of Olive Schreiner* by Cronwright Schreiner (London 1924); *Not Without Honour* by Vera Buchanan Gould (Cape Town 1948); and *Olive Schreiner* by Ruth First and Ann Scott (London 1980). The quotation on p. 127 is from the Cronwright Schreiner biography.

The other works by Olive Schreiner referred to are:

Dreams (London 1890)

Trooper Peter Halkett (London 1897)

A Letter on the Jew (Cape Town 1906)

Woman and Labour (London 1911)

Thoughts on South Africa (London 1923)

From Man to Man (London 1926)

Undine (London 1929)

16.) Adapted from the Introduction to *From a Land Far Off: A Selection of South African Yiddish Stories* (The Kaplan Institute, University of Cape Town 1987) edited by Joseph Sherman. The extract from H.M. Jacobson's unfinished autobiography, is taken from a chapter first published in *The New Review*.

17.) Adapted from an article first published in *The Listener*.

Evelyn Waugh: reported to me by an acquaintance of the novelist.